THE BREVITY OF LIFE

THE BREVITY OF LIFE

How to Make the Most of the Time God Gives You

BY
PHILIP J. GENTLESK

Xulon Press
2301 Lucien Way #415
Maitland, FL 32751
407.339.4217
www.xulonpress.com

ISBN-13: 978-1-6628-1836-3
Hardcover ISBN-13: 978-1-6628-1837-0
Ebook ISBN-13: 978-1-6628-1838-7

DEDICATION

*T*his book is dedicated with love and pride to my three children, Phil Jr., Michael and Mary, and to my lovely wife of 52 years, Mary. Words can never begin to express how much I love you all.

TABLE OF CONTENTS

CHAPTER ONE

LORD, LET ME KNOW HOW TRANSIENT I AM

Why, you do not even know what will happen tomorrow. What is your life? You are a mist that appears for a little while and then vanishes." — James 4:14

D o you ever wonder when you're going to die?

Or what's going to happen to you when you do?

If not, then you can quit reading this book right now. Simply put it down, turn on the TV and check out what's showing on Netflix, Hulu or Apple TV.

But I warn you that sooner or later, you will be in your sixties – and if you are in your sixties now, you will be in your eighties – and wondering, "What became of my life?"

You may be wondering whether you spent time doing the things you really needed to do. Did you spend too much of your life working when you should have been enjoying the company of your spouse, or playing with your children and grandchildren? Did you fritter away the hours when you could have been involved in something that really mattered?

And here is the biggest, most important question you can possibly ask yourself:

Have I spent enough time preparing for the moment when I will leave this world?"

In other words:

"Have I invested enough time getting to know God – and serving Him?"

Let me go back to the first question I asked at the beginning of this book. Do you ever wonder how and when you're going to die? Because the truth is you **are** going to die. Everyone does. And even though death seems like a very scary and horrible thing, it's quite natural. Death happens every single day. There are literally hundreds of ways to die, and none of us know how or when our day will come.

The famous screenwriter/actor Woody Allen once said, "I don't want to achieve immortality through my work. I want to achieve immortality through not dying." That makes us laugh because it's absurd. It just doesn't work that way. Or does it? More about that a little later. By the way, although millions of people know that Allen quote, most of them don't know the second half of it. "I don't want to live on in the hearts of my countrymen," Allen said. "I want to live on in my apartment."[1]

Sorry Woody, that's not going to happen.

The fact that death is commonplace is shown by the fact that most local newspapers carry a regular obituary section. The one in the newspaper I read has gotten larger recently. It used to be that one page was quite enough to record all the passings of people in our community, but these days it often takes at least two pages – and sometimes three. I have a suspicion that this may be largely

---

[1] Woody Allen, "The Illustrated Woody Allen Reader," edited by Linda Sunshine (London; Jonathan Cape) 1994

due to COVID-19, which, as of this writing, has taken the lives of an estimated 520,000 people here in the United States.

It is a sobering experience to read the obituary page because it reminds you that everyone dies. This has been true ever since the first human beings brought sin into the world. More about that later. It is also sobering because you see productive lives of 70 or 80 years described in a few lines of copy. It's disheartening in a way, to see all those years of struggle, tragedy and triumph reduced down to a few paragraphs.

The late Actor George Burns, who lived to be 100 years old, often said, "The first thing I do when I get up in the morning is check the obituaries. If I'm not in there, I go ahead and make breakfast." That's a funny line, but guess what? George Burns eventually wound up on the obituary page, as will all of us.

In the biblical book of Psalms, the great King David writes:

> *"Show me, Lord, my life's end*
> *and the number of my days;*
> *let me know how fleeting my life is.*
> *You have made my days a mere handbreadth;*
> *the span of my years is as nothing before*
> *you.*
> *Everyone is but a breath,*
> *even those who seem secure."*
> —*Psalm 39:5-6*

Even though most of us may not want to think about the day of our death, it is vitally important to be prepared. You might think of death as being like a very long journey. No one would set out on a three-week vacation without preparing for it. You must have a suitcase full of the clothes you'll need. You must also pack items like toothpaste and a toothbrush, important medicines, and a map or a guidebook. And don't forget to take along enough money to complete the trip, make hotel reservations at the cities you're going to visit, and so forth.

Why then, would anyone embark on a journey that will last forever without being prepared? That is madness! And please don't view death as a leap into the dark. There is absolutely no need to do that! It is possible to be prepared, and that's why I'm writing you today.

The Bible assures us that there is no need to fear death — if we are prepared. And how do we prepare? The gospel of John explains this:

> *"For God so loved the world, that He gave His only Son, that whoever believes in Him should not perish but have eternal life."*

> *—John 3:16*

There it is in a nutshell. The man, woman or child who believes in the Son of God has no reason at all to fear death. When Jesus rose from the dead on the very first Easter Sunday, He opened the doors to eternal life in Heaven for all humankind.

As the book of 1 Corinthians says:

> *"When the perishable has been clothed with the imperishable, and the mortal with immortality, then the saying that is written will come true: "Death has been swallowed up in victory."*

> *"Where, O death, is your victory?*

> *Where, O death, is your sting?"*

*The sting of death is sin, and the power of sin is the law.
But thanks be to God! He gives us the victory through
our Lord Jesus Christ. – 1 Corinthians 15:54-56*

This is good news, indeed. But I want to draw your attention to two very important parts of the verses we've just discussed. First, notice that John 3:16 says that whoever believes in Jesus will not perish. Eternal life is contingent upon our belief in the Son of God, but the reverse of this is also true. Anyone who does not believe in Jesus will perish.

And this verse is not talking about merely giving intellectual assent to the truth that Jesus is the Son of God. To believe in Jesus means to accept the truth that He paid the penalty for your sins, and to believe that He was telling the truth when He said, *"I am the way and the truth and the life. No one comes to the Father except through me." (John 14:6)*

The book of 1 John also says, *"Whoever has the Son has life; whoever does not have the Son of God does not have life." (1 John 5:12)*

For the person who believes, the sting of death has been removed, but as John 3:33 says, *"Whoever believes in the Son has eternal life, but whoever rejects the Son will not see life, for God's wrath remains on them."*

The last thing I mean to do is bring you down or depress you. I am not sending you bad news, but good. There is no need for you, or anyone else, to die. When you belong to Jesus, what the world calls "death" is really just a move from this world to the next. One minute, you are in this world full of trouble and sorrow, and the next you are in a paradise where there are no tears, no pain, no broken hearts, no diseases, no wars or terrorist acts. In an instant you cross from this "veil of tears" to a land where you will never be able to wipe that smile off your face, no matter how hard you try!

Chapter Two

The Meaning Of Life

"I hated life, for the work which had been done under the sun caused me only great sorrow; for all is futility and chasing after the wind."

—Ecclesiastes 2:17

I t's the age-old question. People have been asking it for thousands of years, and if the Lord delays His coming, they will be asking it for thousands more:

"Does my life have meaning?"

How do you feel about this? Do you ever wonder if your existence has a purpose? Are human beings just a random collection of atoms that will all float away in different directions when we die – or are we an integral part in some great design?

For the answers to these questions, let's turn to Solomon, the great king of Israel, who lived approximately 3,000 years ago. Solomon was a man noted for his wisdom. In fact, the Bible tells us that when Solomon was about to ascend to the throne, God told him that he could have anything he wanted, and instead of asking for great riches, Solomon asked for the wisdom he needed to be a good ruler. God was so pleased with this request that He gave Solomon the wisdom he had asked for, along with great wealth.

We know that Solomon's reputation had spread all over the known world, because the Queen of Sheba traveled over 1,000 miles to Jerusalem, a journey that would have taken about six months, to see Solomon's kingdom for herself. When she did, she said, "The half has not been told."

Among his many great achievements, Solomon presided over construction of the great temple in Jerusalem.

If anyone should have felt that he had a full and meaningful life, it should have been King Solomon.

Even though God had blessed him in many ways, he began to wonder if there wasn't something more. What happened to Solomon?

The great tragedy was that he eventually allowed his great riches to tempt him away from God. He began to seek meaning in the things God had given him, rather than in God Himself.

His sins were many, including idolatry. He married many foreign women and allowed his wives to construct statues of their false gods in different locations throughout Jerusalem.

Despite all he had been given, it was Solomon who wrote the depressing words from the book of Ecclesiastes recorded at the top of this chapter. Ecclesiastes is Solomon's record of his search for meaning. At no time during the writing of this book does Solomon speak for God. Instead, he uses the word "I" 87 times. The experiences he talks about were all constructed from a platform of selfishness.

Solomon, who calls himself "the preacher," set out to experience all that life had to offer. He says, "I gave my heart to seek and search out by wisdom concerning all things that are done under Heaven." You might say he became the world's biggest pleasure-seeker. His approach was strictly carnal, selfish, and physical. His perspective was here and now. This view is completely compatible with his spiritual status at the time he wrote this book.

He knew that he had compromised his integrity before God, and that God was angry with him. He felt that all he had to look forward to was death. Solomon's conclusion was that this life by itself cannot give anyone lasting happiness — and he was right on target. He had lost the one thing in the world that was most precious to him – his relationship with God.

Solomon's value system was not right! His perspective conflicted with God's perspective. He had been a mighty king, but he became an example of pride and arrogance.

Ecclesiastes is unique among the books of the Bible. It demonstrates how man's heart longs for answers, while at the same time glorifying in its selfishness. It calls our attention to the inevitable— trouble, evil and the monotonous cycle of life. It asks questions the rest of the Bible answers: How did we get here? Does life have meaning? Why are we here, and does the work we do matter? Why does the world often seem to be devoid of justice? What happens after we die? Does life have any meaning?

The answer to that last question is that life has meaning because God is Life. His existence brings purpose to everything.

Every human being should pay attention to the conclusion Solomon reaches after his long search for the meaning of life:

"Now all has been heard;
here is the conclusion of the matter:
Fear God and keep his commandments,
for this is the duty of all mankind."
—Ecclesiastes 12:12

Solomon concludes that it is our relationship with and obedience to God that gives purpose to life – and I agree.

Admittedly, Ecclesiastes is a difficult book to understand. One is left wondering how someone who was so close could wander so far away from Him. And yet, it happens all the time. The Old

Testament is full of accounts of kings who spent most of their lives serving God, but who turned to idolatry toward the end of their lives. In our own day, we have seen well-known pastors seduced into extra-marital affairs and other sins, although I am not going to name any names.

A study of Ecclesiastes requires discernment and thought. I believe that God's purpose in having this book in the Bible is to show us the futility of "chasing after the wind." He wants men and women to store up rewards in Heaven, not on earth.

Think about all you have accomplished during your earthly life. You may have made a lot of money, won honors, or built yourself a mansion to live in. But do you really think that anyone will care about those things ten years after you have left this world behind?

Consider the celebrities who are in the news every day. We hear about all the money they have donated to charities, their unbelievable homes in multiple places, their opulent lifestyles, and on and on. None of this will be able to buy them an extra second of time when God calls them to give account of themselves. You may remember what happened a few years ago, when the United States was plunged into a great recession. Our government stepped in to save some corporations like General Motors because they were considered "too big to fail and die." Well, some celebrities may feel that they are too famous and too important to die, but they are wrong. Elvis Presley is dead and gone. Ditto Frank Sinatra and two of the Beatles. Princess Diana, Mother Teresa, and Billy Graham are all dead. Everyone dies, without exception, saints and sinners alike.

In the book of Ecclesiastes, Solomon describes how he pursues pleasure. He describes how hard he worked as king, how many possessions he amassed, all the homes and beautiful gardens he had, all his slaves and concubines, and all the gold and silver piled up in his bank account. These possessions made him happy for a short time, but then the happiness faded away and he decided all his pursuits were just "chasing the wind." He finally decided that, no matter what, it is better to be wise than a fool.

At this point, he finds himself in despair. Why? Simply because he could not find the meaning of life. For Solomon, the bottom line was that all his efforts were in vain and that vanity even pursues a man while he sleeps. Solomon comes to the conclusion that there is nothing humans can do except enjoy the gifts God has given us, which he describes as working, eating, drinking, and resting.

Solomon says God has designated a proper time for things to occur and put "eternity" into our hearts—a limitless past and future that we cannot understand. Time keeps moving on, he says, and men and women must find something creative to do to fill their time on earth.

Next, Solomon moves on to oppression. Basically he says that because of oppression and sadness, man is better off dead. Then he makes an interesting statement:

"Therefore I praised the dead who were already dead."

What does he mean by this? There are the dead who are in their graves, and then there are those who are biologically alive, but walking around with a dead spirit. Then he says, "Better than both is he who never existed, who has not seen the evil done under the sun."

What a pessimistic view of life! Especially for one who was born into such privilege and power. But this is what happens when we refuse to obey God's laws and won't live the way He wants us to live.

You can see that what I said earlier is true: Ecclesiastes is an unusual and most difficult book to understand. It is full of hopeless despair. No praises, no peace, only questionable behavior on the preacher's part.

In Chapter two of his book, Solomon touches on the single largest stumbling block for mankind, which is pleasure. He is determined to find out if pleasure can bring him the meaning his mind and heart crave.

The answer is no.

At the end of his pleasure experiment he declares that laughter is madness and that pleasure accomplishes nothing. (Ecclesiastes 2:2) He again judges it to be vanity, useless and meaningless. He assures us that the life that is lived without an eternal perspective is futile. So the question is not the existence of God, but whether or not God matters.

In these modern times, most people rarely think about death. They are too busy trying to live life to the fullest, to squeeze out all the pleasure that life has to offer. Most of us live in a way that shows our belief in the words of an old beer commercial we used to hear on TV: "You only go around once in life, so grab for all the gusto you can." But as Solomon warns us, this is an unrewarding, and eventually self-destructive, way to live.

Through his personal experiences, Solomon shows us that all earthly goals, pursued as ends in themselves, lead to disappointment and emptiness. The highest goal in this life is obeying God!

Although, as we've already said, Ecclesiastes can be rather depressing and distressing, it also has many important truths to teach us.

In Ecclesiastes we learn that God made everything appropriate in its time and that He set eternity in man's heart. In other words, the "I will live forever button was installed," and God told us to rejoice and do good in our lifetime. He gave us simple gifts like delicious food, clear, cool water, satisfying labor and so on.

Now consider what you see today. Luxury houses, luxury cars, athletes and entertainers who are over-indulged as well as many,

many everyday individuals who live in million-dollar homes and who drive luxury cars to their beach houses. Welcome to America 2021! Man is not thinking of eternal treasures, even though Jesus tells us not to lay up treasures for ourselves here on earth, but rather in Heaven, where thieves don't break in and steal. (Matthew 6:19) We must learn from Solomon that peace of mind does not come from earthly wealth.

He also teaches us not to allow our speech to cause us to sin. In the fifth chapter of Ecclesiastes, he writes:

> *"Do not be quick with your mouth,*
> *do not be hasty in your heart*
> *to utter anything before God.*
> God is in Heaven
> *and you are on earth,*
> *so let your words be few.*
> *A dream comes when there are many cares,*
> *and many words mark the speech of a fool.*
> *(Verses 1-3)*

Most of the book of Proverbs was also written by King Solomon, and we find similar words in the tenth chapter of that book:

> *"Sin is not ended by multiplying words,*
> *but the prudent hold their tongues."*
> *(Proverbs 10:19)*

How many times have you said something that you regretted as soon as it was out of your mouth? If you have no regrets about anything you've said, then you are a wise person, indeed. James, the brother of Jesus, writes:

"The tongue is a small part of the body, but it makes great boasts. Consider what a great forest is set on fire by a small spark. The tongue

also is a fire, a world of evil among the parts of the body. It corrupts the whole body, sets the whole course of one's life on fire, and is itself set on fire by Hell. All kinds of animals, birds, reptiles and sea creatures are being tamed and have been tamed by mankind, but no human being can tame the tongue." (James 3:5-8.)

Jesus said that when the day of judgment comes, we will all have to give account of every empty word we have spoken. (Matthew 12:36) I don't know about you, but this is pretty scary to me. I hate the thought of standing before God and trying to explain some of the things I've said. And, because life is so short, I know the Judgment Day will be here before we know it.

But here's the good news. Those who have accepted Jesus Christ as their Lord and Savior have been cleansed of their sins. In other words, Jesus has declared us "not guilty," and we have no sins to confess on Judgment Day, including the mean and evil words that may have come out of our mouths. We are no longer guilty because we have been "justified" by Christ's blood. And, as the country preacher explained, justified means "just as if I'd never sinned."

Another very important fact can be found in Ecclesiastes 7:1:

> *"A good name is better than fine perfume,*
> *and the day of death better than the day of birth."*

The meaning of the first part of this verse seems obvious. A good man leaves behind a good reputation. Thus, people honor the efforts of his life. The good man or woman is honored by the people of his or her community.

But why does Solomon say that the day of death is better than the day of birth? There are several reasons. First of all, you may have many problems in this life, and Solomon implies that they will all disappear when you die. This is certainly true for the one who belongs to Jesus.

Going to a funeral is a sad experience, of course, but it teaches us that we all must die and face judgement. Therefore, a man who wants to know about Heavenly rewards understands that the day of his death is more desirable than the day of his birth. The fear of death has been removed by the resurrection of Christ.

In the seventh chapter of Ecclesiastes, Solomon asks some important questions that are still relevant today. How is it that the wicked of this world often seem to live such blessed lives? They seem to be so healthy and wealthy while good people can't seem to catch a break. The answer, of course, is that God does not look at the world through the same lens we use. He looks beyond outward appearances and into the heart. He knows that many of those who appear to have it all in this life are actually miserable deep down inside. This is borne out by the number of "beautiful people" who decide to end their lives every year. They want us to believe that they are happy and satisfied, but this is obviously not true.

Think about it for a minute. Do you believe what you read on Facebook or other forms of social media? On Facebook, everybody seems to be having a great time. Their children are the most athletic, smartest and best-behaved you'll ever meet. Their vacations are spent in unimaginably beautiful places. Their daily lives are filled with excitement and adventure.

Have you ever wondered why your life can't be like that? Perhaps because it isn't real – or at least much of it isn't real.

The important thing to remember is to keep our eyes on God, and not our neighbor's success. Comparing ourselves with others is never helpful. Remember the last of the Ten Commandments:

> *"You shall not covet your neighbor's house. You shall not covet your neighbor's wife, or his male or female servant, his ox or donkey, or anything that belongs to your neighbor." (Exodus 20:17)*

Another thing to keep in mind is that God has an eternal perspective. He knows that this life is only a short trial run for the real life, which is to follow. If you are a baseball fan, you might think of your life here on earth as being like Spring Training for the real season, which is yet to come. No one in his or her right mind would exchange an eternity of pleasure for a few good years here on earth.

Jesus told a parable about a beggar named Lazarus, who spent his days outside the gate of a rich man's estate. He was covered with sores but received no medical attention. He was so hungry, he would have been delighted to have a few crumbs that fell from the rich man's table. But he didn't get them. Apparently, the rich man never even noticed the poor beggar.

But when they died, the tables were turned. Lazarus found himself in Paradise, but the rich man was in the flames of Hell. One of the important points of this story is that there is more to life than the few years we spend on this planet. And what we do here will determine what we experience in the next life. Anyone who trades a few good years here for torment throughout all eternity is making a horrendous mistake.

Consider this: Suppose there was a small bird that was flying back and forth across the Grand Canyon, dropping a small pebble into the vast gorge each time he did. By the time that bird had filled the canyon with those pebbles, eternity would have just begun. Again, how could anyone trade that for a few hours, days or weeks of joy here in this temporary world?

1 Kings 11:41 says, *"And the rest of the acts of Solomon, and all that he did, and his wisdom, are they not written in the book of the acts of Solomon?"*

I recently had an opportunity to read a book which is translated from Hebrew and is said to be a copy of "The Acts of Solomon." As I read, I was shocked by some of Solomon's thinking and his actions.

This book says that Solomon became very interested in occult practices. It quotes Solomon as saying things like, "I am beginning to lose any feelings of purpose," and "I do not know what I have become or who I am." Solomon speaks often with his Jinn (genie), a being who is considered, by the ancient Jews, to be one notch below an angel. This book says that Solomon knew all the languages of all the tribes, and even had the ability to communicate with all different types of beasts. Yet he asked, "How can I say that I am free to make my own choice, if the language I speak was given; are my thoughts really even my own thoughts? Or are they someone else's?"

Thus it seems that one of the wisest men who ever lived, wound up in confusion and fear. This is the sad end of the life lived in pursuit of hedonistic pleasure.

Chapter Three

You Are Designed To Live Forever

"He has made everything beautiful in its time. He has also set eternity in the human heart.

– Ecclesiastes 3:11

When God created human beings, His intention was that we would live forever, on a planet that never experienced war, crime, disease, hatred, jealousy, violence or pain of any kind.

I have heard broken-hearted people blame God when their loved ones died, asking how He could allow—or even cause—this to happen. But God is not the one who brought death into this world. The devil did it, and he had plenty of help from the first two human beings. When Adam and Eve disobeyed God, sin entered our world, and as the Bible says, *"For the wages of sin is death, but the gift of God is eternal life in Christ Jesus our Lord." (Romans 6:23)*

Tragically, many Americans feel that they can be saved by living a good life. They are respectful people who don't cause any problems for their neighbors, keep their lawns neatly trimmed, don't throw wild, loud parties on Saturday night, go to church on a regular basis and worship their own gods – gods who don't put any demands on them.

As Paul wrote to his protégé Timothy, *"For the time will come when men will not tolerate sound doctrine, but according to their own desires, having an itching ear, they will gather around them teachers to suit themselves."* The New American Bible says it this way *"...but wanting to have their ears tickled, they will accumulate for themselves teachers in accordance to their own desires."*

The problem is, those man-made, ever-so-friendly gods of ours will fail us in the end. When the last days come upon us, we will find out that they are nothing more than illusions.

In fact, we are already seeing this in these early years of the 21st century.

Not only are we in the midst of a global pandemic, but people all over the world have had to deal with unprecedented flooding, fires, tornadoes, hurricanes, earthquakes, devastating swarms of locusts, tsunamis, etc.

Why? Because this planet has turned its back on her Creator. Unless we repent and return to Him, we will not be able to escape His judgment.

As I look around, I am reminded of a Steve Miller Band song called *"Fly like an Eagle,"* which says, "Time keeps on slipping, slipping, slipping into the future."[2] The future is upon us. It has come faster than any of us thought it would, and it is not the Utopia some thought it would be. The truth is that the world we live in is passing away. A breakdown in the global supply chain will soon appear and the economies of many countries will be shattered as a result.

I recently read an article in the Prophecy News Watch which talked about "The Baltic Dry Index." The Baltic Dry Index is a shipping and trade index created by the London-based Baltic exchange. It measures changes in the cost of transporting raw materials. Over the last 12 to 14 months, this index has basically collapsed — a

---

[2] "Fly Like an Eagle," by Steve Miller, Copyright 1976 by Sailor Music, Tradition Music Company, B Flat Music and Kags Music Corporation

direct result of the Coronavirus pandemic. Now, we have several mutations (variants) of this virus, and only God can help us. [3]

The situation is dire, but it is not hopeless. If you are a church-goer, or if you attended Sunday school as a child, you may remember the story of Jonah, the prophet who was swallowed by a whale (although the Bible doesn't say it was a whale) after running off to sea when God called him to go preach to the people of Nineveh. Nineveh was the largest city of the ancient Assyrian Empire, and was where Mosul, Iraq, is currently located. You may remember that Mosul was very much in the news during the heyday of the vicious Islamic State terrorists.

In Jonah's day, the city was apparently an extremely wicked place. Because of this, God decided that if the citizens of Nineveh didn't change their ways, he would destroy the city, just as He had destroyed the cities of Sodom and Gomorrah many years before.

God told Jonah to go to Nineveh and warn the people what was going to happen if they didn't turn from their sins. Why didn't Jonah do as God asked? Because the Assyrians were Israel's enemy, and he hated them. He would have been happy to see God's wrath poured out on the city.

Well, after his ordeal with the fish, Jonah decided to do what God had asked him to do. He prophesied against the city and, much to Jonah's chagrin, the people repented, including their king.

The third chapter of Jonah says:

"When Jonah's warning reached the king of Nineveh, he rose from his throne, took off his royal robes, covered himself with sackcloth and sat down in the dust. This is the proclamation he issued in Nineveh:

"By the decree of the king and his nobles:

Do not let people or animals, herds or flocks, taste anything; do not let them eat or drink. But let people and animals be covered with sackcloth. Let everyone call urgently on God. Let them give up their evil ways and

---

[3] www.prophecynewswatch.com (Article title and date)

their violence. Who knows? God may yet relent and with compassion turn from his fierce anger so that we will not perish."

"When God saw what they did and how they turned from their evil ways, he relented and did not bring on them the destruction he had threatened." – Jonah 3:6-10

Jonah wasn't happy, to put it mildly. He just knew this was going to happen, and that's why he hadn't wanted to go to Nineveh in the first place.

There are many lessons to be learned from the story of Jonah, but the main point I want us to see is that God is merciful. As 2 Peter 3:9 says, *"The Lord…is patient with you, not wanting anyone to perish, but everyone to come to repentance."*

No matter what you may have done, if you repent – which means to turn away from your sins – and ask God to forgive you, He will. And once he does, you no longer have to fear death because you know it is nothing more than a step into the Kingdom of Heaven.

Just remember, it's not a prayer that saves you, but Jesus Christ, who gave His life for yours. You can trust yourself to His care, knowing that He will keep you safely in the palm of his hand.

CHAPTER FOUR

WHAT DOES THE BIBLE SAY ABOUT THE END OF LIFE?

"Show me, LORD, my life's end
and the number of my days;
let me know how fleeting my life is.
You have made my days a mere handbreadth;
the span of my years is as nothing before you.
Everyone is but a breath,
even those who seem secure." – Psalm 39:4-5

What would you do if you knew you were about to die? If the doctor told you that you had, say, six months left, how would you spend your time? Would you go out and try to make as much money as possible as quickly as possible? Or would you look for ways to bless as many people as possible so you could leave this world knowing that you had made a positive difference in other people's lives?

The truth, of course, is that we are all about to die. You, me, and everyone we know. Perhaps not in six or nine months. But even if you live another 50 or 60 years, that – as we've seen – is only a drop in the bucket of eternity.

This is a sobering thought, of course. But it shouldn't scare you. If you have prayed to accept Jesus, the closer you get to death, the closer you get to Paradise. That is something to look forward to, like opening the brightly wrapped presents under the tree on Christmas morning.

I have seen quite a few news articles recently talking about how scientists are looking for ways to increase the human lifespan. Some are suggesting that within the next 25 years or so, it may be common to see human beings live for 150 years, or even longer. Suppose that these predictions are correct. What if we reach the point where an average life expectancy is 200 years? The truth is that this is only a matter of a few minutes when contrasted with the length of eternity.

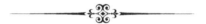

Do you remember those WWJD bracelets that were so popular in the 1990s? You saw them everywhere in those days, and I wish they were still as popular now as they were then. WWJD stood for "What would Jesus Do?" The bracelets were meant to motivate their wearers to stop whenever they faced a decision and to think about what Jesus would do in that situation.

I think this is a very good idea for those who are contemplating their own mortality. What would Jesus do if He were facing death? To find the answer, let's take a look at what He did.

First and foremost, He spent time in the scriptures. Pastor Greg Laurie writes, "Most American homes have a Bible, but ironically, fewer than half of all American adults can name the four gospels." He also talks of a program which found that, "Most participants could name the four Beatles, but they could not name one of the Ten Commandments. It gets worse. Twelve percent of American adults thought that Joan of Arc was Noah's wife and half of graduating high school seniors thought Sodom and Gomorrah were husband and wife."[4]

The next thing Jesus did as he approached His death on the cross was minister to people, helping them any way He could. He was constantly working to help others receive and enjoy the benefits of the kingdom of Heaven. Look how He ministered to His apostles during the Last Supper, just before He was arrested by Roman soldiers in the Garden of Gethsemane. He washed their feet. (John 13:5) He reassured them that life goes on beyond the grave and that He was going away to prepare a place for them. (John 14:2-3) He preached the gospel to them, reminding them that He was the way, the truth and the life. (John 14:6)

Jesus never looked at worldly things, but rather sought to build Heavenly rewards. It's important to check your motives at all times. Do nothing out of pride or greed. Never forget that after you die there will be no trailers full of your belongings following the hearse! The old cliché is right on. You can't take it with you. You store up Heavenly treasures by helping others, not by focusing on yourself.

If you haven't already done so, I suggest you develop an "eternal perspective." When you get out of bed each morning, the first words out of your mouth should be, "Thank you, Lord. I'm yours all day today. Use me to help others in your name." If you sincerely ask Him to use you, He will. I have been amazed by the opportunities He puts in my path when I am sincerely seeking His will. If you haven't discovered this for yourself, try Him and see.

Jesus also spent time in prayer. The last thing He did before Judas betrayed Him with a kiss was fall to His knees in the Garden of Gethsemane and discuss the situation with His Heavenly Father. It wasn't easy. He was in such turmoil that He sweat great drops of blood. But He managed to yield Himself to the Father's will.

---

[4] "Marked for Life," by Greg Laurie, harvest.org/resources, November 7, 2020.

Christ didn't want to go to the cross. Of course not. His humanity fought against the very idea. Crucifixion is one of the slowest and most painful forms of execution ever devised by the evil heart of man. Imagine the pain of having large nails driven into your feet and hands. Then hanging there for hours, gasping for every breath, until you eventually suffocate. It was a horrible way to die. But our Lord knew that His father was in complete control and that He had to obey in order to offer Himself for the sins of all humankind and bring reconciliation between God and man.

Remember, nothing can happen in this universe that is not allowed by God. He is in complete control.

But God is not capricious or vengeful. He loves us more than we can ever imagine. In His eyes, no price is too great to pay to save the human soul. The human body will die and decay. But the soul will live on forever. The soul is precious beyond what any of us can imagine, and that is why the book of Proverbs says, *"The fruit of the righteous is a tree of life, and he who is wise wins souls." (Proverbs 11:30, NKJV)* How can we win souls? By telling others about Jesus and the eternal life He offers.

But before we can tell others about the peace and satisfaction that Jesus brings, we have to understand it for ourselves. Jesus interceded for man, pouring Himself out unto death, and it is imperative that we experience His amazing love.

When you begin to understand the importance of the soul, then you realize how important it is to tell your family, friends and neighbors about Jesus. As you probably know, the motto of the Boy Scouts is "be prepared." This should also be the motto of everyone who knows Jesus as Lord and Savior. Be prepared to tell others about the abundant life Jesus offers. Be prepared for the arguments they will use in order to put off responding to His invitation to come to Him. Be prepared for angry retorts from people who don't want to hear the gospel. (Please don't let your fear of angry responses keep you from doing what it takes to save souls from Hell.)

As the apostle Paul wrote to his young protégé, Timothy:

"Preach the word; be ready in season and out of season, reprove, rebuke, exhort, with great patience and careful instruction." (2 Timothy 4:2)

Some of the excuses you may hear:

1) I am not a sinner.

2) I am too big a sinner and have no hope.

3) I am not a hypocrite who goes to church on Sunday and raises holy hands to God, and then will rob you blind on Monday.

4) How could a loving God send people to Hell?

5) I can't believe in God because there is too much evil in the world.

Let's take a closer look at some of these objections.

First, for the person who insists that he or she is not a sinner. The book of Romans tells us clearly, *"...all have sinned and fall short of the glory of God, and all are justified freely by his grace through the redemption that came by Christ Jesus." (Romans 3:23-24)* There has only been one human being in all of history who did not sin, and that person was Jesus Christ our Lord.

Next, the person who says he or she is beyond redemption. In 1 Timothy 1:15, the apostle Paul says, *"Christ Jesus came into the world to save sinners—of whom I am the worst."* Furthermore, Jesus Himself said, *"Whoever hears my word and believes him who sent me has eternal life and will not be judged but has crossed over from death to life." (John 5:24)*

Thirdly, the person who says there are too many hypocrites in church. It is true that there are hypocrites mixed in with those who are truly striving to live for Jesus. But there are bound to be hypocrites at your favorite restaurant. Will you stop eating there because of this? Will you stop cheering for your favorite team because there are hypocrites among the fans? Remember the old saying that the church is a hospital for sinners rather than a museum for saints. It's good that there are hypocrites in church, hearing the good news of the gospel. This is exactly where they need to be.

Next up is the one who says he can't believe in a God that would send people to Hell. But the truth is that God doesn't send anyone to Hell. The person who winds up there has made his or her own choice in the matter. If you jump off the top of a skyscraper, you are going to die when you smash into the street below. That's because you can't fight the law of gravity. If you chain smoke cigarettes all your life, despite all the warnings about the harmful effects of tobacco, you are likely to die of lung cancer. You have disobeyed the laws of health. And if you insist upon turning your back on God, you are going to wind up in Hell after you die. This is a natural consequence of a life of disobedience.

Would you expect to see someone like Adolf Hitler in Heaven? I don't think so. How about Josef Stalin, or Pol Pot, or a serial killer like Ted Bundy, who murdered over 30 young women? Again, I don't think so. As we've already discussed, the human soul is immortal. So there has to be some place where evil people can spend eternity, and that place is Hell.

God does not want to see anyone sentenced to eternity in Hell. In fact, 1 Peter 3:19 says that Christ went and preached to "the spirits in prison." He gives us every opportunity to avoid Hell.

This leads us to the person who says he can't believe in God because there is too much evil in the world. Why have there been so many despots, serial killers and other evil people? Why do we experience deadly hurricanes, earthquakes, floods, fires and other natural disasters? Why do we have to suffer from diseases like COVID-19?

I believe the person who asks these questions is looking at life through the wrong lens. A better question might be, where does good come from? How about the beauty we see all around us? Where do the heroes come from who sacrifice their lives for others? Who put it into the hearts of medical doctors to spend their lives in poor communities in Appalachia, helping the poorest of the poor, or bringing healing and hope to people in the world's poorest communities in Africa, Asia or Latin America? Where did a mother's love for her child originate? Or the fiery beauty of a sunset, far out on the Western horizon?

I believe that all of these things are a representation of the love of God. They are a reflection of His character. Our world was corrupted by sin, but not completely corrupted. Examples of God's love and goodness remain all around us.

In his book, *Mere Christianity*, C.S. Lewis writes, "If you do not take the distinction between good and bad very seriously, then it is easy to say that anything you find in this world is a part of God. But, of course, if you think some things really bad, and God really good, then you cannot talk like that. You must believe that God is separate from the world and that some of the things we see in it are contrary to His will. Confronted with a cancer or a slum, the Pantheist can say, 'If you could only see it from the divine point of view, you would realize that this also is God.' The Christian replies, 'Don't talk damned nonsense.' For Christianity is a fighting religion. It thinks God made the world – that space and time, heat and cold, and all the colours and tastes, and all the animals and vegetables, are things that God 'made up out of His head' as a man makes up a story. But it also thinks that a great many things have gone wrong

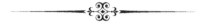

with the world that God made and that God insists, and insists very loudly, on our putting them right again." [5]

At some point, we have to stop asking questions like, "Why is there evil in the world," and decide to let God handle the matter. If we decide that we won't believe in God until all of our questions are answered, then we will never believe in God.

Do you understand how the process of digestion works? I don't, but I know it's a real and vital thing. The same is true of photosynthesis. How do plants transform sunlight into chemical energy that produces food? This one is way beyond my pay grade, but I see it happening all around me on a daily basis.

Here's another one. I don't have the slightest idea how antibiotics fight illness. I'm sure my brother Mike knows this because he's a doctor who has helped thousands of patients over many years.

I am grateful that God gave me the ability and knowledge to build a successful business, but there is so much I do not know. Even the most intelligent person can't understand everything.

In the same way, there is much about God and how He runs the universe that I don't understand. But I trust Him. In fact, with every year that passes, I trust Him more.

When it comes to faith in God, you eventually have to say, "I believe" and take a leap into the darkness. When you do, it won't really be darkness at all because He will be there to catch you and He is the Light of the World. And the more you trust, the more He makes His presence known.

---

[5] CS Lewis, "Mere Christianity," (New York; Harper Collins) 1952

CHAPTER FIVE

How Does God Want Us To Live?

*"Be very careful then how you live – not as unwise,
but as wise..." Ephesians 5:15*

What should you do once you have decided that Jesus alone holds the key to abundant eternal life and have accepted His offer of salvation? How do you obey the Bible's command to "be careful how you live?" Or, as the King James Version, puts it, "walk circumspectly, not as fools, but as wise."

- **First and foremost** you should live out your beliefs. Any and all who come in contact with you must see Christ. As 1 Corinthians 4:9 says, *"We have been made a spectacle to the whole universe, to angels as well as to human beings."* Others are looking at us, whether or not we realize it. These include our children, our neighbors, our co-workers, our friends, our brothers and sisters, and people we don't even know. Our behavior may attract them to Christ, or it may repel them. Pray that God will enable you to live in such a way so that you do the former.

- **Second, you must love all people.** You cannot fake love. If you find it difficult to love someone, then pass it on to the Lord and allow Him to love through you. Ephesians 4:32

tells us, *"Be kind and compassionate to one another, forgiving each other, just as in Christ, God forgave you."* Jesus also said that the world would know that we are His followers by the way we love each other. (John 13:35) Are we living up to that? If not, we must let it begin with us.

- **Third, take the I out of your conversations**, and by all means avoid the technicalities — in other words avoid the individual who is radical in his or thinking. Focus on the needs of others.

Remember, do not cast your pearls to pigs! Your role is to present Christ. As John the Baptist said, *"He must increase, but I must decrease." (John 3:30, King James Version)* Remember that God is not here to serve us. Rather, we are here to serve Him. Finally try to get the picture in your head that there is a Heaven, there is a Hell, and you get to choose where you go. Your choices, every choice matters! God is real and He loves you.

- **Fourth, pray for discernment**. (James 1:5) Also, help bring the person to a decision. Make it crystal clear that there is a difference between knowing God and knowing about God. James 4:8 tells us that if we draw near to God, He will draw near to us. That reminds me of a sign I saw in front of a church years ago. It read, "If God seems far away, guess who moved." How do we draw near to God? By talking to Him every day in prayer, both sharing what is on our hearts and asking Him to share His heart with us.

It seems to me that most Christians seem to think that payer consists of talking to God, and it's true that's part of it. But any relationship would be very one-sided if you only talked but never listened. If you've ever been in a relationship like that, you know how frustrating it can be. No one enjoys being in a relationship with a person who talks about himself all the time.

Still, it can be difficult to learn how to listen to God. You may fall asleep once or twice while you're sitting in silence before the Lord. But that's okay, because there are few things in life that can be more soothing than falling asleep in our Father's arms. And if you keep listening, you will begin to hear His voice.

Another way you can move closer to God is to spend time in His Word every day. Soak yourself in God's Word. Meditate on it, letting it sink into you spirit. And then, strive to walk in obedience to what it says.

- **Fifth, live every day as if it were your last.** Treat everyone as you want to be treated. Say the words your loved ones need to hear from you. Let your friends know you appreciate them. If you have an unresolved issue with someone, try to resolve it. And most importantly, say yes to Jesus.

Before we end this chapter, I want to remind you again that death is inevitable. There are only two people in the history of this world who have not died: Enoch who "walked with God," and Elijah, who went to Heaven in a chariot of fire. I think of so many people who insisted that they did not believe in God, and then they were called to stand in front of him.

John Lennon was emphatic in his atheism. He famously said that the Beatles were more popular than Christ. He also said that he expected Christianity to disappear completely in the near future. He didn't know that he would be shot down at the age of 40 and have to give an account of himself to God.

Recently, famous radio/TV host Larry King passed away. His passing was not a huge surprise, really, since he was 87 years old. But like Lennon before him, King was an avowed atheist. Just think. He had nearly nine decades to prepare to meet God, but he didn't do it.

I also think of Christopher Hitchens, author of the best-selling book, *God Is not Great*, which presented his case in favor of atheism. By all accounts, Hitchens was a brilliant thinker. He had been raised in a "nominally Christian" family, but later became one of the world's foremost proponents of atheism. The subtitle of his book was "How Religion Poisons Everything," which is a clear expression of his attitude toward people of faith. Despite his sharp criticism of organized religion, and especially Christianity, Hitchens became something of a favorite of evangelical Christians, many of whom were praying for his salvation.

In 2010, Hitchens was diagnosed with advanced esophageal cancer. I wouldn't be so bold as to say that this was a warning from God, but I do believe it could have and should have been a wake-up call. He knew that, unless God intervened, he was nearing the end of his life. God had given him an opportunity to rethink his point of view.

Many Christians wrote to let him know they were praying for his healing and salvation. Prayer services were held in his behalf. Hitchens described the prayers as "a nice gesture that is fine by me,"[6] but he was not otherwise moved by them. In fact, he told friends not to believe it if they heard that he had experienced a death-bed

---

[6] "Christians pray for atheist Christopher Hitchens," Christianity Today.com, September 22, 2010

conversion. Hitchens was a stalwart atheist to the end, which came to him in December of 2011 at the age of 62.

Hitchens' younger brother Peter is a Christian and author of several books, including *The Rage Against God*, which was published in 2010, a year before Christopher's death. Peter, who often jousted publicly with his brother over his anti-religious views, read a passage from the book of Philippians at Christopher's funeral.

What can we learn from Christopher Hitchens, Larry King and John Lennon? That even though we may all argue and protest against it, we all have our date set to meet with God. We don't know when it will come, but God does, and its arrival is certain. This is the time, today is the day, to accept the righteousness that Christ offers. Only then can we know for sure that we will someday hear our Father say, "Well done, thou good and faithful servant."

Chapter Six

Learning To Walk In Obedience

"We ought to obey God rather than men." Acts 5:29

A s we have seen, once you have accepted Christ as your Lord and Savior, you must begin living out a life of obedience—not out of duty, but because you love Him and want to please Him. And not because you are saved through obedience, for you are saved the moment you surrender your life to Christ. But obedience brings the great satisfaction of knowing you are following His will for you and that His favor will rest upon you.

The Bible tells us that obedience is better than sacrifice. (1 Samuel 15:22) In other words, God values our obedience above everything else. In the time of the prophet Samuel, the Israelites thought they could get away with just about everything, as long as they offered up the burnt sacrifices God commanded. But they were wrong. As God said: *"These people come near to me with their mouth and honor me with their lips, but their hearts are far from me."* *(Isaiah 29:13)*

Your obedience is a demonstration of several important characteristics regarding your life in Christ.

First, obedience demonstrates your faith. As 1 John 2:3-6 says: *"We know that we have come to know him if we keep his commands. Whoever says, 'I know him,' but does not do what he commands is a liar, and the truth is not in that person."*

Obedience also demonstrates our love:

"This is how that we know that we love the children of God; by loving God and carrying out his commands." (1 John 5:2)

And obedience brings blessing. For an example of this, look at the blessing God pronounces upon Abraham in the 22ⁿᵈ chapter of Genesis:

> *"The angel of the LORD called to Abraham from Heaven a second time and said, 'I swear by myself, declares the LORD, that because you have done this and have not withheld your son, your only son, I will surely bless you and make your descendants as numerous as the stars in the sky and as the sand on the seashore. Your descendants will take possession of the cities of their enemies, and through your offspring all nations on earth will be blessed, because you have obeyed me.'" (Genesis 22:15-18)*

Obedience is an act of worship. True Christian obedience flows from a heart full of gratitude. I think one of the best ways to learn how important obedience is to God is to read the first nine verses of Psalm 119.

> *"Blessed are those whose ways are blameless,*
> *who walk according to the law of the LORD.*
> *Blessed are those who keep his statutes*
> *and seek him with all their heart—*
> *they do no wrong*
> *but follow his ways.*
> *You have laid down precepts*
> *that are to be fully obeyed.*
> *Oh, that my ways were steadfast*
> *in obeying your decrees!*
> *Then I would not be put to shame*

> *when I consider all your commands.*
> *I will praise you with an upright heart*
> *as I learn your righteous laws.*
> *I will obey your decrees;*
> *do not utterly forsake me.*
> *How can a young person stay on the path*
> *of purity?*
> *By living according to your word."*

The apostle Paul reveals his heart in 2 Corinthians 7:1:

> *"Therefore, since we have these promises, dear friends,*
> *let us purify ourselves from everything that contami-*
> *nates body and spirit, perfecting holiness out of rever-*
> *ence for God."*

I've mentioned before that I could never begin to understand how men can exchange the vast joys of eternity for fleeting pleasures here on earth. Jesus said, *"What good will it be for someone to gain the whole world but forfeit their soul?"* (Matthew 16:26) But we are not talking about trading your soul for the whole world, but rather trading it for one fleeting pleasure that will be over in five minutes or less. People have not changed that much since Esau sold his birthright for a bowl of stew. Momentary satisfaction is not the solution to unhappiness, but rather the birth of additional troubles.

Danish philosopher Soren Kierkegaard said that the problems of humankind were boredom, anxiety, and despair. He believed that boredom was a particular nuisance and must be avoided at all costs. He also taught that conflicts between one's ethical duty and one's religious duty were detrimental to spiritual health and a major cause of anxiety – and that this conflict between the finite and infinite produced despair.

The good news is that both boredom and anxiety can be eliminated if you have complete faith in God. This is not merely checking the boxes of going to church, volunteering for church duties, etc. It takes intense personal commitment to serve a living God, but knowing that He is real and that He loves you is the glue that holds you together.

And yet, what much of the world looks for today is 'Pleasure without Conscience.' If it feels good do it, they say, and to heck with the consequences. But the Bible warns us, *"Do not be deceived: God cannot be mocked. A man reaps what he sows." (Galatians 6:7)*

The late Stephen R. Covey, author of "Seven Habits of Highly Effective People" also wrote about what he considered to be the seven most deadly sins.[7] They are: 1) Wealth without work 2) Pleasure without conscience. 3) Knowledge without character. 4) Business without ethics. 5) Science without humanity. 6) Religion without sacrifice. 7) Politics without principle.

You can certainly see the problems that each of these situations would bring about. Let's take a closer look:

1) **Wealth Without Work.** Of course, it's not really a sin to be born into a wealthy family. But someone who has great wealth without working for it may never understand the importance of hard work, nor the fact that money is like fertilizer. It is only beneficial when you spread it around. As we learned from the story of Solomon, great wealth is not a guarantee of happiness in this life, or in the life to come.

---

[7] Stephen R. Covey, "Principle-Centered Leadership," (New York: Free Press) 1992

2) **Pleasure without conscience**. Solomon sought after pleasure without thinking about the consequences, and it left him empty and depressed. He wrote that "the sleep of a working man is sweet." (Ecclesiastes 5:2) I believe that this is because the hard-working man or woman feels a sense of satisfaction about what he or she has done. They know that they have earned their reward of a good rest. The person who chases after pleasure over everything else, and doesn't care what it costs, pays a great price. Whatever "rewards" he finds in this lifestyle will pass quickly.

3) **Knowledge without character**? Have you ever known anyone who fit this description? I think of all those technical wizards who have put their skills to work stealing people's identities, or hacking into their computers and then asking them to pay huge ransoms to get their files back. Some have shut down computer systems for hospitals and other critically needed organizations. They don't care who they hurt or what damage they cause. They may get away with it in this life. But not in the life to come.

4) **Business without ethics**. We have all seen the pitfalls of this particular "sin." The United States was thrown into a recession by the shenanigans that were taking place in the banking industry a few years ago. Thousands of mortgages were given to families who had no way to pay them off. The whole thing was like a Ponzi scheme that was bound to collapse – and it did. Prior to this, we saw a number of big companies go bankrupt because they inflated their bottom lines and lied about their profits. Remember WorldCom and Enron? I do. And I'm reminded of a parable Jesus tells in the 12th chapter of Luke.

The protagonist in the story is an extremely successful farmer who decides he is going to tear down his barns and build even bigger ones to house all his wealth. Then, he will take it easy for the rest of his life, thinking about nobody but himself:

"But God said to him, 'You fool! This very night your life will be demanded from you. Then who will get what you have prepared for yourself?' This is how it will be with whoever stores up things for themselves but is not rich toward God." (Luke 12:20-21)

The business owner who doesn't have a well-developed sense of morality may succeed for a short while. But his or her final destination is sure to be failure and disgrace. As we've already seen, God is not mocked. Nor is he fooled.

5) **Science without humanity.** When I hear this phrase, my mind goes immediately to the horrors that took place in Nazi Germany. Hitler's scientists were determined to build a master race, and they were willing to do the most awful "experiments" to get there. People were tortured, mutilated and killed – all in the name of science. Science without humanity is science without a conscience, and that can be a monster.

What does this have to do with the afterlife? I believe that God expects us to speak out against injustice where we see it. I also believe He wants us to speak out on behalf of life. We must not allow ourselves to be persuaded that it's okay to act against human life simply because science says it's okay, or because science makes it seem like the "intelligent" thing to do. For example, when I was a young man, abortion was against the law. Everyone knew that killing an unborn child was wrong – the taking of a human life. But now, for the most part, abortion has been given society's stamp of approval. Science and politics have combined to make abortion seem acceptable. It is no longer considered to be a murder, but rather a procedure, and it is commonplace. But this is wrong!

And now, we are hearing about euthanasia and right-to-die laws. If we think we are too intelligent and learned to care about what God thinks, we are mistaken. This is just one more area where our obedience is required.

6) **Religion without sacrifice.** If your religion doesn't cost you anything, then it may not be worth anything. For many Americans, belonging to a church is not much different than belonging to a social club. They go to a church on Sunday morning where they sit on plush pews as comfortable as those in any theater, listen to inspiring music and encouraging sermons, put a few dollars in the plate when it comes around, and then go home feeling good about themselves.

Now, the last thing I want to do is criticize what other Christians do. But I really think God expects His people to give until we have to do without some things we'd really like. Sometimes he expects us to give up that big game or favorite TV program so we can spend more time in prayer. Listen to these lyrics from Casting Crowns song *Start Right Here*:[8]

"We want our coffee in the lobby.
We watch our worship on a screen.
We got a rock-star preacher,
Who won't wake us from our dreams.
We want our blessing in our pockets.
We keep our missions overseas,
But for the hurting in our cities,
Would we even cross the street?"
"But we wanna see the hearts set free
and the tyrants kneel,
The walls fall down and our land be
Healed,
But church if we want to see a change
in the world out there.
"It's got to start right here.
It's got to start right now.
Lord, I'm starting right here.
Lord I'm starting right now."

Jesus said that some people who think they are obeying Him, really aren't. *"Not everyone who says to me, 'Lord, Lord,' will enter the kingdom of Heaven, but only the one who does the will of my Father who is in Heaven. Many will say to me on that day, 'Lord, Lord, did we not prophesy in your name and in your name*

---

[8] "Start Right Here," performed by Casting Crowns, written by Bernie Herms, Matthew West, John Mark Hall and Set Mosley, Copyright 2018 by Highly Combustible Music, House of Story Music, One 77 Songs, Works by Pure Note Songs, Xeva Music, Essential Songs, My Refuge Music, Centric Songs, and These Songs Go to 11

drive out demons and in your name perform many mir-
acles?' Then I will tell them plainly, 'I never knew you.
Away from me, you evildoers!'" (Matthew 7:21-23)

It's not always easy to be obedient. Since man is born with a sin nature, and we are all pleasure seekers to some degree, it takes hard work and self-sacrifice to become obedient. God expects us to put our hearts and souls into it.

7) Politics Without Principle. I was talking with a friend recently who has spent her entire life in politics—serving on various boards and committees in her community. She said that she has seen a number of people go into politics with good intentions. They really wanted to make a difference in the world. But then, as they gained power, they were approached by people who needed favors and were willing to pay big sums of money for them.

Sadly, when this happened, many of these politicians gave up their youthful ideals. They started worrying more about lining their pockets than they did making the world a better place.

We need committed Christians in local, state and national politics — people who are determined to walk in obedience no matter what the cost. In fact, this is not only true of politics. We need obedient, faithful, Christ-followers in every area of endeavor: In business, education, law, medicine, the church, the media, and especially in the home.

Being obedient to God involves using your time wisely. I heard one preacher say that God expects us to tithe both our time and money. In other words, give 10 percent of our income to God's work, and spend 10 percent of our time in godly pursuits, such as praying, reading the Bible, doing good works in Jesus name, fellowshipping with other believers, etc.

There's nothing in the Bible that says this is true. Then again, the scriptures do make it clear that God expects to be our top priority. Consider that there are 168 hours in a week. One tenth of that would be 16.8 hours. So if you tithe your time to God it comes out to 2.4 hours per day. And that includes time for church on Sunday and a small group during the week.

Remember, this is not a "command," or even a suggestion. I'm just giving you something to think about. My point, really, is that some of us fritter away a lot more time than this, and we all need to consider how God wants us to use the time He has given us.

What do you enjoy doing? Perhaps you like to play golf, go bowling, see movies, attend sporting events, go out dancing, or just finding a quiet spot to read a good book. None of these things are bad for you. In fact, they are all fun and offer exercise for the mind and body. And I'm sure you can think of many more wholesome activities that people like to do.

You may be surprised to find out, as I was, that people have been playing games and indulging in other leisure-time activities for thousands of years. For example, people in Egypt were playing board games (like checkers) as far back as 3,000 years before the birth of Christ. Wrestling and boxing were also big in Egypt, for athletes and spectators.

Some 500 years before Christ, polo was invented in Persia, followed closely by hockey. The apostle Paul compares the Christian life to running a race and winning a prize, (1 Corinthians 9:24) so we know that such events were common throughout the Roman Empire. The list goes on and on, full of games and other events to relieve the boredom (typical of that experienced by Solomon). The problem occurs when we become obsessed with such activities, or when they become our top priority, taking the place that rightly belongs to God.

The Lord says, "Be still and know that I am God." (Psalm 46:10) Man says "Keep me busy with mindless things so I won't be bored." But who can be bored if he, or she, has a vibrant, fulfilling relationship with God?

It is certainly okay to enjoy a pastime. Just be careful not to turn it into an idol. It takes trust to become obedient, but trust in what or whom? In other words how does trusting help you in the area of obedience to God? (Proverbs 3:5-8)

God expects to hold first place in your life. And He deserves it, too. After all, we are here because of Him. He is our creator who gave us life. When your passion for your personal interests supersedes your interest in things of the Lord, you have created an idol.

According to the latest studies, it takes an average of 66 days to develop a new habit.[9] Satan and his demons are adept at bringing dangerous new habits into the lives of those who have let their attention wander from their creator. They may start off by trying to get a "toe-hold." Once this is established they move on to the process of getting a 'foothold.' Then, finally it becomes a 'Stronghold.' Once this is in place, without God's intervention, you are doomed. So don't let the devil get that toe-hold in the first place!

A good example of this is someone who begins drinking socially. Soon, he reaches the point where he enjoys a drink or two with his friends every day. Then he gets to the next step, where he is drinking every day, and he doesn't care if his friends are around or not. Alcohol has its hooks in him and the toehold has become a stronghold.

---

[9] PsychCentral.com, October 17, 2018, "Need to Form a New Habit, Give Yourself at Least 66 Days," by John M. Grohol, Psy.D

If you get trapped by a bad habit, and you have surrendered your life to Jesus, you can ask him to break your sinful habit and He will honor your request.

Keep in mind that once you are saved it is God's responsibility to sanctify you. After we are saved, we become participants in the Lord's school of obedience. More often than not, the path we are on is unclear and our destination is unknown. We must continue to walk in faith. Your friends may wonder what happened to you, because they think you've changed. And they're right! You are no longer the person you used to be! You would rather attend church or read your Bible than listen to mindless chatter about the National Football League or the latest major golf tournament.

You're different because you are bound for glory! You're on your way to Heaven, where you'll see the Lord and be reunited with your friends and loved ones who've gone on before you. Perhaps you've heard that Buddha said, "It is better to travel well than to arrive." This has been paraphrased as "The journey is more important than the destination." Well, forget it, because that's not true for you. If you belong to Jesus, your destination is Heaven, and there is absolutely nothing that could be better than arriving there.

CHAPTER SEVEN

YES, THERE IS AN AFTER LIFE

"He has made everything beautiful in its time. He has also set eternity in the human heart; yet no one can fathom what God has done from beginning to end."–Ecclesiastes 2:11

The vast majority of humans have always believed in life after death. In the United States, a poll undertaken by *60 Minutes* and *Vanity Fair* magazine found that 80 percent of Americans believe in the afterlife – and the vast majority of these believe in the biblical concept of Heaven and Hell. Actually, only 13 percent of Americans said they didn't believe that life would continue on after death, because 7 percent said they didn't really know.[10]

You might argue that some Eastern religions don't believe in the afterlife, but that's not quite true. While Buddhists believe that the aim of existence is to quench personal desires — in other words, to achieve Nirvanna — they also believe that people may need to be reincarnated several times before they achieve this. It seems to me that in order to believe this, Buddhists must also believe that the self lives on beyond the grave. In fact, even though devout Buddhists will tell you that they don't believe in an immortal soul,

---

[10] Ropercenter.edu, "Paradise Polled: Americans and the Afterlife," accessed March 20, 2021

they do speak of several Heavens for faithful Buddhists who have accumulated good karma in this life. However, these Heavens are not permanent and are not real, but illusion, like all the world around us.

Now, I'm no expert on Buddhism. And please don't think I'm defending a belief in reincarnation. I'm not. I believe that the Bible book of Hebrews is correct when it says: "…people are destined to die once, and after that to face judgment." (Hebrews 9:27) If we don't accept Jesus this time through, we're not sent back for another chance. It's now or never. And actually, if we belong to Jesus, there is no judgment, because we have already been declared not guilty, and are living eternal life.

My point in talking about this is to show that all human cultures – past and present – have had a strong belief in an afterlife. Where did they get this belief? From God, the one Who put eternity in their hearts.

Let's take a brief look at what some ancient societies believed about life after death:

1) **Mesopotamia**: The religious leaders in this ancient land described Hell as a distant land of no return, where the dead dwell without rank or merit. They are housed and sealed in a fortress, typically with seven gates barred against invasion or escape. It was believed that everyone went to Sheol when they died, where they ate clay and drank bad water. For the most part, the Mesopotamian afterlife is a glorified extension of their experiences on earth.

2) **Egypt:** The ancient Egyptians also believed that the afterlife would be a continuation of life here on earth. But there

was a huge problem. The dead person had to undergo a dangerous underworld journey before being granted entry into the world beyond this one. The Egyptians believed so strongly in this journey that they mummified their "dearly departed," and outfitted their tombs with all they would need for their trip. And even if you made the journey safely, that was no guarantee that you would be allowed into Paradise. First, you had to have your heart weighed by the Feather of Truth. If sin was detected, the traveler's heart would be devoured by demons.

3) **Greece:** The ancient Greeks believed that all people went to the same place when they died, and that was Hades, the land of the dead. Hades was viewed as a place consisting of good and bad neighborhoods. The Greeks always imagined civilized life on this earth connected to a city. Thus, they felt the same way regarding their afterlife. When Odysseus visited Hades in the Odyssey of Homer he saw his friend, King Achilles, who remarked that he would rather be a slave on earth than a king in Hades.

4) **Rome:** Ancient Romans believed that upon death, the deceased would meet up with Mercury (Son of Jupiter), and be taken to the river Styx. There he or she would pay the ferryman (Charon) a fee to cross the river. Once they crossed the Styx, they were met and judged by Rhadymanthas, Aenaeus and Minos. Because they couldn't get across the river without paying the ferryman, people were buried with a coin to pay the crossing fee.

5) **Iran:** Adherents of Zoroastrianism believed that this world is a struggle between the Ahuras (gods of light) and the Daevas (demons of darkness). The Zoroastrian Hell is

presided over by Yima, the first victim of death. The demons who dwell there take much joy in torturing sinners, but not forever. At the end of time, Hell is destroyed with the restoration of Ahura Mazda's good creation.

6) **The Ancient Levant:** The Levant is made up of countries such as Lebanon, Palestine, Jordan, Iraq, Syria that are bounded by the Mediterranean Sea in the west, the Arabian Desert in the south and Mesopotamia to the east. In each of these countries it was thought that the dead person would reach his or her destination in the afterworld by taking a trip across a lake, river or other obstacle.

Another common belief was that there is a place of punishment that can be found beneath the earth. Residing there are demons, ghosts, and sinners. The punishment to be endured there corresponds to sins committed during the dead person's lifetime. In each civilization, Hell is pictured as a dark, dreary cavern located deep underground. Interestingly, whether you are speaking about the Levant, or Africa, Greece, Rome, etc., they all have one thing in common: Pain and suffering from which no one can ever escape.

There is good news, though, and that is that Jesus, who was God in the flesh, took our punishment upon Himself so we don't have to worry about going to a terrible place of pain and punishment after we die. He has paid for our "ticket" to Paradise.

One important question we might ask is, "Why are all these versions of the afterlife so similar?" Why do so many cultures believe in a dark and dreary underground where sinners will pay the price for the evil deeds they committed while they were among the living?

Why do so many believe in the existence of a bright, happy paradise where righteousness will be rewarded?

One good explanation for this is that all these beliefs had their origins in a truth that came from God Himself. But as various cultures moved away from God, the truth became twisted and distorted. The basic framework remained, but the details of what God had taught were lost.

It was like that game kids play, where some "secret" is whispered down a line from one child to another and then repeated by the child at the end of the line. Almost always, the "secret" this child shares has nothing at all to do with what the first child said.

In my book, *Don't Miss the Celebration in Heaven*, I share how distortions were brought into the teachings of the Roman Catholic Church over the centuries. The basic truth of salvation through faith in Christ is still there, but it is almost hidden by all the man-made additions and changes to the simple message of the gospel.

I believe that there is only one God, and that He is the creator of every person on this earth. At one time, all cultures knew Him and His laws, but that has changed. Today, there are hundreds of different teachings, but most retain at least a small portion of truth. I find it interesting that when explorers from Europe encountered the Mayan people in what is now Mexico, they discovered that the Mayans had the same basic beliefs about a place of punishment far beneath the earth that received the souls of the unrighteous dead, and a Paradise where righteous men and women would enjoy comfort and plenty forever.

How could these people, separated by oceans from Europe, Africa and Asia, have the same basic beliefs that were common in these faraway lands? I believe this is just one more reason to believe that all of these beliefs came from a common source — a truth that all people knew when the world was new.

This reminds me of the book, Eternity in their Hearts,[11] written by missionary Don Richardson. During his years in New Guinea and other parts of the world, Richardson found that many tribes and cultures were ready to accept the gospel because they had been prepared by their wise men and prophets. They knew somehow that men would come to bring them back to the truths they had once known, but had forgotten.

For example, Richardson tells of what happened in the 1880s when various groups in Asia were waiting for a messenger to come to them from the one God Who created everything. These people believed this messenger would bring them the holy book they had lost, so they could be reconciled to God. They were overjoyed when missionaries came, bearing Bibles.

This is a reminder that there are hundreds of cultures in this world of ours, but there is only one God and Father of them all. As Paul wrote to Timothy, "For there is one God and one mediator between God and mankind, the man Christ Jesus, who gave himself as a ransom for all people." (1 Timothy 2:5-6)

---

[11] Don Richardson, "Eternity in Their Hearts," (Ventura, Ca.; Regal Books) 1981

CHAPTER EIGHT

YOU HAVE A DECISION TO MAKE

"Then Agrippa said to Paul, 'You almost persuade me to become a Christian.'" Acts 26:28. NKJV

Have you ever made a decision that you regret?
That's a dumb question. Of course you have. We all have. Every one of us has turned left when we should have turned right, said "yes," when we should have said, "no," or vice-versa, or made the decision to buy something we really couldn't afford.

I want to start this chapter by telling you about two men who, I believe, made the worst decisions anyone could ever make.

The first was a king named Agrippa. His full name was Herod Agrippa II, and he was the eighth and last of the Herods to reign over Judea. He was the great grandson of Herod the Great, who ruled in Jerusalem when Jesus was born, and ordered that every male under two years old in the town of Bethlehem be put to death.

Late in the apostle Paul's life, he was on trial in Caesarea under Festus Porcius, who was the Roman procurator (or governor) over Judea. Festus felt that Paul had really done nothing wrong and was conflicted about how to handle his case. When he shared Paul's story with the king, Agrippa said, *"I also would like to hear the man myself."* (Acts 25:22)

The very next day, Paul was brought before the king and governor and asked to testify.

52

The Bible says, *"When Agrippa and Bernice (the queen) had come with great pomp, and had entered the auditorium with the commanders and the prominent men of the city, at Festus' command Paul was brought in. And Festus said: 'King Agrippa and all the men who are here present with us, you see this man about whom the whole assembly of the Jews petitioned me, both at Jerusalem and here, crying out that he was not fit to live any longer. But when I found that he had committed nothing deserving of death, and that he himself had appealed to Augustus, I decided to send him. I have nothing certain to write to my lord concerning him. Therefore I have brought him out before you, and especially before you, King Agrippa, so that after the examination has taken place I may have something to write. For it seems to me unreasonable to send a prisoner and not to specify the charges against him."* (Acts 25:23-27)

After the king gave Paul permission to speak, the apostle told of how he had been a devout Jew who hated Christians and had been convinced "that I should do all that was possible to oppose the name of Jesus of Nazareth." (Acts 26:9)

Paul went on to tell how he had met Jesus as he had traveled along the road to Damascus, on his way to persecute Christians there.

"About noon, O king, as I was on the road, I saw a light from Heaven, brighter than the sun, blazing around me and my companions. We all fell to the ground, and I heard a voice saying to me in Aramaic, 'Saul, Saul, why do you persecute me?'

"Then I asked, 'Who are you Lord?'

"'I am Jesus, whom you are persecuting.'"

He then went on to tell how Jesus told them that he would be sent as God's witness to the Jews and the Gentiles.

When Festus heard this, he cried out to Paul, "Your great learning is driving you insane."

Agrippa's response was different. The New King James Version puts it this way: *"Then Agrippa said to Paul, 'You almost persuade me to become a Christian.'*

And Paul said, "I would to God that not only you, but also all who hear me today, might become both almost and altogether such as I am, except for these chains." (Acts 26:28-29)

King Agrippa had come to a crossroads in his life. He had an important decision to make, and he made the wrong one. He chose against Jesus and the eternal life that Jesus offers.

There is an old song, written many decades ago (in 1871 to be exact) by Philip Paul Bliss, that refers to this tragic moment: Here are the first and last stanzas of this 150-year-old song:[12]

> *"Almost persuaded, now to believe.*
> *Almost persuaded, Christ to receive.*
> *Seems now some soul to say,*
> *'Go Spirit go Thy Way.*
> *Some more convenient day*
> *On thee I'll call.'"*
> *"Almost persuaded, harvest is past!*
> *Almost persuaded, doom comes at last!*
> *Almost cannot avail;*
> *Almost is but to fail;*
> *Sad, sad that bitter wail,*
> *'Almost, but lost!"*

There comes a point in every life where we must make a decision for or against Christ. We must choose wisely – for Christ, and eternal life in Heaven. We cannot afford to make the same mistake that the last Herod made nearly 2,000 years ago.

In the 19th chapter of the book of Matthew, we find the story of the rich, young ruler, who also made a terrible mistake. This young man came to Jesus and asked what he had to do to inherit eternal life. Jesus told him to keep the Ten Commandments, which

---

[12] "Almost Persuaded," by P.P. Bliss, 1871, Public Domain

obviously came as a huge relief to the young man, who said that he had kept them since he was a boy. Then he asked, "What else do I still lack?"

Jesus answered, "If you want to be perfect, go, sell your possessions and give to the poor, and you will have treasure in Heaven. Then come, follow me."

"When the young man heard this, he went away sad, because he had great wealth."

Just think. If he had done as Jesus said, his name would be known by every Christian today. Undoubtedly, he would have become one of the great leaders of the church. Right up there with Peter, Paul and John. But he made the wrong decision, choosing earthly wealth over the abundant eternal life that Jesus offers.

Like the Rich Young Ruler, and King Agrippa after him, we all must choose what we will do with Jesus. Will we accept Him and the love He offers and live forever? Or will we reject His love and descend into eternal darkness.

No one can get away with not deciding. The person who tries to do that is actually deciding against Jesus.

The Bible tells of a challenge the great leader Joshua put before the Israelites: *"Choose for yourselves this day whom you will serve, whether the gods your ancestors served beyond the Euphrates, or the gods of the Amorites, in whose land you are living. But as for me and my household, we will serve the Lord."* (Joshua 24:15)

"Then the people answered, 'Far be it from us to forsake the LORD to serve other gods! It was the LORD our God himself who brought us and our parents up out of Egypt, from that land of slavery, and performed those great signs before our eyes. He protected us on our entire journey and among all the nations through which we traveled. And the LORD drove out before us all the nations, including the Amorites, who lived in the land. We too will serve the LORD, because he is our God."

Did you know that He wants to be your God, too? He wants to bless you as He blessed the Children of Israel, to bless you and see you prosper. Listen to this list of blessings He promises in the book of Deuteronomy:

> *"All these blessings will come on you and accompany you if you obey the L*ORD *your God:*
>
> *"You will be blessed in the city and blessed in the country.*
>
> *"The fruit of your womb will be blessed, and the crops of your land and the young of your livestock—the calves of your herds and the lambs of your flocks.*
>
> *"Your basket and your kneading trough will be blessed.*
>
> *"You will be blessed when you come in and blessed when you go out.*
>
> *"The L*ORD *will grant that the enemies who rise up against you will be defeated before you. They will come at you from one direction but flee from you in seven.*
>
> *"The L*ORD *will send a blessing on your barns and on everything you put your hand to."* (Deuteronomy 28:2-8)

At the end of the day we are all on a journey. Different paths lie in front of you, so which one should you take? Every path is different and full of surprises. But Jesus tells us, *"My sheep hear my voice, and I know them, and they follow me..."* Listen and you will hear the voice of the Master.

When Jesus walked the earth as a man, God spoke to us through Him. After the cross, God did not abandon us. He sent His Holy Spirit to guide us through the troubled waters that come with the storms of life.

Jesus said, "*... the Advocate, the Holy Spirit, whom the Father will send in my name, will teach you all things and will remind you of everything I have said to you.*" (John 14:26) Make no mistake, God is in control. Nothing happens in this world without His approval.

When you are living in complete submission and obedience to God, your life will be an exciting adventure, both now and in the world to come. Where does that adventure begin? I believe it begins on your knees in prayer. I remember that the Christian band Petra once released a song with the lyrics, "Get on your knees and fight like a man." I really like that. The strongest any of us can ever be is when we are on our knees, speaking to our Heavenly Father.

I recall hearing that the famous evangelist Dwight Moody said that he started every day by spending an hour on his knees in prayer – unless he knew that he was facing an especially tough and busy day. Then, he spent two hours in prayer. It sounds counter-intuitive, I know. Most people who are facing a busy day might cut their prayer time short to save time. But that's not how God's economy works. Instead, he works it out so that the more money you give to His kingdom, the more money you have left over. And the more time you give to Him, the more he stretches what you have left so you can get more done! But don't take my word for it. Try it and see!

The next thing I believe you should do is consider your talents and desires and see how God wants you to use them. I believe you will find that God has put certain things on your heart that are like signposts for you to follow. My brother Mike is a great example of this. When we were youngsters, he always wanted to help others. As far back as I can remember, he had a desire to become a doctor. And a fine doctor he is. After graduating from Georgetown Medical School he went on to specialize in pulmonary medicine.

My sister, Maryjane, also chose to go into medicine, becoming a nurse.

Remember that you must listen to your own heart, and not follow someone else's desire for you. My brother and sister did very well in the biology, chemistry area, while I seemed to do well in math and statistics. Most likely, God's purpose for you involves the things you are presently good at. Needless to say my brother and sister went on to bring physical healing to many people, while I went on to build a business in the food sector where the Lord sent many a worker.

So through God our company grew and many men and women became able to care for their families. God knew what he had in store for me, yet I fought Him at the starting gate. I wanted to go to Georgetown Law School. My application warranted a waiting-list only candidate. The Vietnam War was in high gear, and many young men wanted to stay in school because it was the only way to avoid the draft—and a stint on the battlefield.

Two people at Georgetown were a great blessing to me. Chuck Devlin and my brother Mike. Without their encouragement and guidance I would have had a more difficult time. But, as Proverbs 11:14 says, "For lack of guidance a nation falls, but victory is won through many counselors."

In other words, God will direct the right people in your life to properly guide. In the end, trust God. Tell Him you will submit to His will for you. You can always be sure that He knows what He's doing. As Proverbs 3:5 says, "Trust in the Lord with all your heart and lean not on your own understanding..."

If you are a new believer, this may be easier said than done. But as you learn to trust God in small matters, you will learn how to trust Him in bigger situations that have a great deal riding on them.

When I was a young man, I had a fear of flying. Did I fly? Yes. Did I like to fly? No! Flying made me feel out of control and triggered panic in me. Or did I simply fear death? Either way it was very stressful. But as I aged and spent more time with the Lord reading my Bible, I realized I had no control over anything. I also realized that fear was not a product of Love. As a matter of fact, the Bible says, *"There is no fear in love. But perfect love drives out fear..."* (1 John 4:18) I put my faith to the test in 1988 by boarding a plane bound for Israel. There, my wife Mary and I spent three weeks visiting many of the biblical sites we had previously only read about. I basically said, "Lord, we are in your hands not the pilot's hands. It's your plane and we are visiting Your home." We had an absolutely marvelous trip.

Since then, I have been on other flights, including a trip to Europe for Mary's sixtieth birthday. I confess that I am still not comfortable with being 30,000 feet off the ground, but I do not fear flying the way I once did. I have learned that:

1) **God is in control of all things**. Nothing goes on or gets done on earth unless the Lord allows it.

2) **Our understanding of the situation is limited,** but God always has a plan. He is continually in the process of molding us (sanctifying us) in preparation for meeting Him.

3) **Our present comfort is not a priority for God.** But He will always have our backs.

4) **And most important,** to have Christ's peace, you must surrender your life to Him. Do not think for one minute that you lose yourself when you surrender to Jesus. All you lose is the turmoil which is a byproduct of sin.

5) **Reading your Bible daily** will increase your trust in Jesus. Scripture is the backbone of peace. You will come to understand that the Lord keeps His promises. You will now be able to understand this world, its religions, its politics, its ultimate doom.

6) **Finally, you must learn to live** under God's rules. Obedience reaps spiritual blessings and peace. Disobedience culminates in turmoil and confusion, ultimately leading to death and destruction. Take refuge in the fact that God is in control.

CHAPTER NINE

CONSEQUENCES OF UNBELIEF: HELL IS A REAL PLACE

"Do not be afraid of those who kill the body but cannot kill the soul. Rather, be afraid of the One who can destroy both soul and body in Hell."

— Matthew 10:28

I n 2010 my brother-in-law, Ed, wrote and asked me if Hell really exists. I began my response by saying, "Make no mistake, Jesus believed in a literal Hell."

Many people ponder the same question. According to the Bible, Hell is a real place. Do you know there are over 162 references to Hell in the New Testament with over 70 attributed to Christ?[13]

The Bible is clear that, upon death, our souls—our spirits—depart from our bodies (Genesis 35:18) and either ascend to Heaven or descend to Hell.

"And many of them that sleep in the dust of the earth shall awake, some to everlasting life, and some to shame and everlasting contempt" (Daniel 12:2 KJV).

---

[13] "The Truth About Hell"; Terry Watkins; www.gvsu/edu/Hell, accessed March 25, 2021

"Then they will go away to eternal punishment, but the righteous to eternal life" (Matthew 25:46).

When Christians (those who have believed on the Name of the Lord Jesus Christ and accepted Him as Lord and Savior) die, they are immediately taken to Heaven to be with the Lord. We will be absent from our bodies but present with the Lord (2 Corinthians 5:8).

Luke 16:22 records that, upon his death, angels carried the beggar Lazarus to Abraham's side.

Those who have not trusted in the Lord will descend to Hell.

Numbers 16:32-33 tells us, *"and the earth opened its mouth and swallowed them up, and their households, and all the men who belonged to Korah with their possessions. So they and all that belonged to them* **went down alive to Sheol***; and the earth closed over them and they perished from the midst of the assembly."*

Sheol, in the Old Testament, means "the grave." The Hebrew word for Sheol was translated into Greek as "Hades" (Luke 16:24). The punishment of Hades includes burning, loneliness, memory convictions, thirst, and unbearable stench. **Gehenna** is also translated as Hell or lake of fire. Gehenna most probably relates to the Valley of Hinnom, a dumping ground in the city of Jerusalem, a place of filth, stench, fire, and eternal punishment.

What had these people done to provoke the Lord to send them directly to Hell?

Korah, Dathan, and Abiram, and approximately 250 men, rose up against Moses and Aaron. Korah and Moses were related, and Korah and his family had been charged with carrying the most holy things of the temple. Korah and his men confronted Moses saying, *"You have gone too far! The whole community is holy, every one of them, and the LORD is with them. Why then do you set yourselves above the LORD's assembly?"*

Korah was not content with what God had given him and with his assignment from Moses even though it was an honor.

Korah rebelled and accused Moses and Aaron in front of 250 of his followers.

His accusation was false as Moses did not see himself above the community. He had not aspired to the position of leader but had been called by God. Moses knew Korah's rebellion was rooted in ingratitude. He and his followers were not thankful for what God had given them or done for them. As a result, God rebuked their pride and self-seeking ways.

Korah's co-conspirators, Dathan and Abiram, would not meet with Moses, showing disregard for Moses' position and authority. God caused the earth to open up and swallow them, and He destroyed the 250 men with fire.

What was their fate? Matthew 3:12 tells us there is an unquenchable fire. Luke 16:19,24 describe a place of memory, remorse, and unquenchable thirst. They were met with misery and pain.

Many scholars believe Hell is located at the center of this earth. Science supports this possibility. The Smithsonian Magazine's Smart News carried an article by Colin Schultz, titled, "The Center of the Earth is as Hot as the Sun." Schultz reports, "... the planet's core is blisteringly hot. In new research, scientists studying what the conditions at the core should be like found that the center of the Earth is way hotter than we thought—around 1,800 degrees hotter, putting the temperature at a staggering 10,800 degrees Fahrenheit. This superheated core, says the BBC, is about as hot as the surface of the Sun."[14]

In Matthew 12:40, Jesus Christ said: *"For as Jonas was three days and three nights in the whale's belly: so shall the Son of man be three days and three nights in the heart of the earth."*

---

[14] https://www.smithsonianmag.com/smart-news/the-center-of-the-earth-is-as-hot-as-the-sun-43631207/accessed March 25, 2021

"In the heart of the earth" certainly sounds like a definite location. However, Jesus' sojourn into Hell was brief as He purposed to go there to take away the keys of death from Satan.

Referring to King David, Acts 2:31 (NASB) records that *"he looked ahead and spoke of the resurrection of the Christ, that He was neither abandoned to Hades, nor did His flesh suffer decay."* This further confirms that Jesus' journey to Hell was brief and that He didn't suffer the torments like those who are consigned to Hell for punishment.

You may be confused by the different words referring to Hell. Some believe Hell is divided into at least four parts:(a) bottomless pit or great abyss; (b) Tartarus—a place of confinement where the angels who sinned in Genesis 6:1-4 are being held until they are finally cast into the lake of fire; (c) Hades: where the souls of lost people are presently confined while they await the final day of judgement; (d) Gehenna: the final place of torment for Satan, demons, and the lost. This is referred to as the place of the second death because there the soul/spirit experience a final, eternal separation from God.

Hell is a place of memory. Individuals will have continued consciousness (see Luke 16:19-31) where their memories will bring to mind all of their thoughts and actions. The rich man knew immediately where he was and remembered his brothers.

Hell is a place of torment. The rich man said, *"I am in agony in this flame."* It is a place of unquenchable fire from which there is no escape. Matthew 13:42 says, *"there will be weeping and gnashing of teeth."* "Weeping and gnashing" certainly refers to grinding one's teeth, but it also reflects the remorse of conscience, the tortured mind, the experience of pain and torment, rage, and black despair. But this statement also reflects the intensity of divine wrath.

In Mark 9:46 (NKJV) Jesus describes Hell as a place, *"Where their worm does not die, and the fire is not quenched."* Jesus is quoting from Isaiah 66:24, which describes the worm feeding forever on the corpses of the dead who transgressed against God in the midst of unending fire.

Revelation 14:10 tells us, "*...and he shall be tormented with fire and brimstone.*" Brimstone is sulfur and, according to an article in Science Magazine (June 2015), is found in the earth's core.[15]

In his article, "The Truth About Hell," Terry Watkins paints a horrifying picture of the reality of Hell.[16] He begins by quoting Hebrews 9:27, "And as it is appointed unto men once to die, but after that the Judgement."

He continues, "As you leave your body — you realize something is happening. You hear a sound ... getting louder and louder ... screaming ... weeping ... wailing. Terror and fear beyond anything you could imagine overtakes you. 'This can't be happening!' you scream. Your nostrils are filling with the awful stench of burning souls. Your face ignites from the heat. Flames are now blazing from your eyes, nostrils, ears, mouth — from every opening in your body, flames are roaring out. Your body is sizzling and crackling from the flames. Your body is now madly thrashing and convulsing from the horrible pain.

"'Why don't I die?' you scream. You begin weeping and gnashing your teeth with the millions. 'When will this pain stop?' But you know it will never stop ... The darkness is so terrifying, it begins engulfing you. You feel something moving in the darkness... something horrible is happening. 'No! No! This can't be happening,' you scream — as your worm is emerging.

"You begin cursing the day you were born. You scream 'Oh God, why didn't you warn me?'"

The truth is that God *has* warned us. Over and over again. Most have heard preachers and evangelists pleading to receive

---

[15] https://www.sciencemag.org/news/2015/06/earth's-core-brimming-brimstone (accessed March 25, 2021)

[16] "The Truth About Hell"; Terry Watkins

Jesus Christ as Savior and Lord. Perhaps you remember reading a gospel tract. Sometimes we cry, "God, don't you care?" but then remember John 3:16, *"For God so loved the world, that He gave His only begotten Son ..."*

Sometimes we say, "God wouldn't allow this if He is a God of love." But John 3:36 tells us, "... he that believes not the Son shall not see life; but the wrath of God abides on him."

And that place of wrath is Hell.

Sadly, despite the many pleadings and warning people hear throughout their lives, many are not interested in life beyond this one. They see seeking pleasure without regard for consequences a more desirable pursuit.

I believe there are varying levels to Hell, as God is fair and just. *"... You reward everyone according to what they have done."* (Psalm 62:12)

Since God is perfectly just, I think punishment will be harsher for those who hear the gospel and purposely disobey, rather than those who disobeyed in ignorance. Even so, the Bible doesn't emphasize whether there are degrees or levels of Hell. Instead, Scripture focuses on avoiding Hell and spreading the gospel to encourage others to avoid it as well.

When we look at our lives on earth, what could we ever accomplish here that would be worth spending eternity in Hell? Christ asked, *"What good is it for someone to gain the whole world, yet forfeit their soul?"* (Mark 8:36)

In his book, "Beyond Death's Door," author Dr. Maurice Rawlings, (a specialist in cardiovascular disease) explains that he was a devout atheist and considered all religions to be hocus-pocus. Until 1977 when his perspective underwent a radical change. Dr. Rawlings had been successful at resuscitating patients who had been declared clinically dead. He describes one such patient who awoke terrified during the procedure.

Rawlings relates that each time the man regained a heartbeat and respiration he screamed, "I am in Hell!" and, petrified, would plead with Rawlings to help him. His grotesque grimace expressed his horror. His pupils dilated, he perspired and trembled. Rawlings writes that the man looked as if his hair was "on end." Then he said, "Don't you understand? I am in Hell. Don't let me go back to Hell!"

"The man was serious, and it finally occurred to me that he was indeed in trouble. He was in a panic like I had never seen before."[17]

Rawlings is not the only one to describe glimpses into Hell. As many well-known, self-professed atheists faced death, their eyes were opened. Their dying words serve as a warning that Hell is indeed real and Jesus Christ is our only salvation.

Voltaire: "I am abandoned by God and man! I shall go to Hell! O Christ, O Jesus Christ!"

Thomas Paine: "I would give worlds if I had them, that 'The Age of Reason' had never been published. O Lord, help me! Christ, help me! No, don't leave; stay with me! Send even a child to stay with me; for I am on the edge of Hell here alone. If ever the Devil had an agent, I have been that one."

I think it's impossible to read the dying words of Sir Francis Newport (head of an English infidel club) and not shudder: "What argument is there now to assist me against matters of fact? Do I assert that there is no Hell while I feel one in my own bosom? That there is a God I know, because I continually feel the effect of His wrath. That there is a Hell, I am equally certain, having received an earnest of my inheritance already in my own breast. Oh! That I was to lie a thousand years upon the fire that is never quenched to purchase the favor of God and be reunited to Him again! But it is a fruitless wish. Millions and millions of years will bring me no nearer to the end of my torments than one poor hour! O Eternity!

---

[17] Maurice Rawlings, "Beyond Death's Door"; (Nashville; Thomas Nelson, Inc.) 1979

Eternity! Oh! The insufferable pangs of Hell! Oh Eternity! Forever and forever!"

Sir Thomas Scott: "Until this moment, I thought there was neither God nor Hell; now I know and feel that there are both, and I am doomed to perdition by the just judgment of the Almighty!"

M.F. Rich: "Terrible horrors hang over my soul! I have given my immortality for gold; and its weight sinks me into a hopeless, helpless Hell!"

Thomas Hobbs: "I say again, if I had the whole world at my disposal, I would give it to live one day. I am about to take a leap into the dark."

Thomas Carlyle: "I am as good as without hope – a sad, old man gazing into the final chasm."

David Hume (atheist famous for his skepticism of religion) cried out on his deathbed, "I am in flames!" A witness said his "desperation was a horrible scene."[18]

Another chilling occurrence is described in a compendium of the "Dying Testimonies of the Saved and Unsaved" compiled by Solomon Benjamin Shaw (1854-1941), a Methodist Episcopal minister, historian, and essayist. This eyewitness account, related to Shaw by B. F. Closson of Bloomington, Nebraska, portrays the futility, hopelessness, and desperation of a woman who rejected the outstretched hand of the Savior until it was too late.

"Mrs. Josie Brown, the subject of this sketch, came under the personal observation of the writer in 1886. I had often urged her to give her heart to God while she was in health, but she refused.

"I called to see her during her last sickness and found her in a most distressing state of mind. She recognized me when I came in, and was loath to let me leave long enough to bring my wife, who

---

[18] https://www.usmessageboard.com/threads/famous-last-words-atheists-on-their-death-bed.374153/ accessed March 25, 2021

was only three-quarters of a mile away; saying, 'Devils are in my room, ready to drag my soul down to Hell.'

"She would begin in a low, measured tone to say, 'It must be done! It must be done!' continuing to repeat the same with increasing force and higher pitch of voice, until she would end with a piercing scream, 'It must be done!'

"Her husband asked her, 'Josie, what must be done?'

"She answered, 'Our hearts must be made right!' And again she would entreat me to take her away, affirming she could see devils all around her.

"She would say, 'See them laugh!' This would throw her into a paroxysm of fear and dread, causing her to start from her bed; but when I tried to get her to look to Jesus for help she said, 'It is no use; it is too late!'

"I trust I shall never be called upon again to witness such a heart-rending death-bed scene as hers. There was more that transpired, but I have tried to make this sketch as brief as possible."[19]

Galatians 6:7-8 reads, "Do not be deceived: God cannot be mocked. A man reaps what he sows. Whoever sows to please their flesh, from the flesh will reap destruction; whoever sows to please the Spirit, from the Spirit will reap eternal life."

Are you living to please your flesh or your spirit?

The Way Out

People often ask how a loving God could create something so horrible for a creation He loves. We must remember that, while God is love, He doesn't love all things. He hates pride, injustice, abuse, murder — all sin. All of mankind deserves Hell, but God provided a way to avoid such punishment.

---

[19] https://www.cuttingedge.org/shaw/shaw22.html#110, accessed March 25, 2021

By sending His only Son to the cross to become our sin and defeat death, God Himself redeemed us. Jesus' death and resurrection provides our entrance into Heaven. Our God loves us enough to punish sin and loves us enough to take our punishment on Himself.

Why Hell Exists

Hell was not made for man but for the devil and his angels. Jesus, in Matthew 25:41, tells us, *"Then he will say to those on his left, 'Depart from me, you who are cursed, into the eternal fire prepared for the devil and his angels."*

The name Satan means 'Adversary'. He is called Lucifer in Isaiah 14:12. He is also called dragon, devil, serpent, Apollyon, Beelzebub, Belial, the father of lies, and prince of this world. He was created as a guardian cherub (Ezekiel 28:15-17). He was full of wisdom, perfect in beauty, the angel who covered God.

Isaiah 14:12-14 (NAS) describes his demise: *"How you have fallen from Heaven, You, star of the morning, son of the dawn! You have been cut down to the earth, You who defeated the nations! But you said in your heart, I will ascend to Heaven; I will raise my throne above the stars of God, And I will sit on the mount of assembly.*[20] In the recesses of the north, I will ascend above the heights of the clouds; I will make myself like the Most High."

Ezekiel 28:14-18 (NASB) further describes the devil saying, *"You were the anointed cherub who covers, And I placed you there… you were blameless in your ways from the day you were created **until unrighteousness was found in you.**"*

---

[20] The Place where God promised to meet with His people Exodus 25:22; 29:42-43

Lucifer was exiled from Heaven when he became filled with violence, and his heart grew prideful because of his beauty. His wisdom was corrupted by his own splendor.

Arguably, the most graphic portrayal of Satan in the Bible is found in Ezekiel 28:18:

"By your many sins and dishonest trade you have desecrated your sanctuaries. So I made a fire come out from you, and it consumed you, and I reduced you to ashes on the ground in the sight of all who were watching."

Satan abused God's blessings. His sin of pride led directly to his punishment. He would be brought to ashes, and it would be made known to all. As he profaned the holy places (sanctuaries), God will profane him.

Lucifer's high status was evidenced by the precious stones that were his covering before his fall. Those stones signified priesthood, as the same stones were found on the breastplate of the high priest (Exodus 28:17-20).

Isaiah 14:11 (NASB) tells us Lucifer had a significant role in the music of Heaven. *"Your pomp and the music of your harps have been brought down to Sheol; maggots are spread out as your bed beneath you, and worms are your covering."*

Lucifer was the anointed cherub who covered the throne, not just a cherub but an anointed cherub. God makes it clear that He established Satan.

But the Bible also describes Satan as a twisted serpent that only God could crush. What happened to Satan to change him from a beautiful angel to a detested being?

Pride was found in him.

And God dealt with him justly by ejecting him from Heaven and casting him to earth.

*"How you are fallen from Heaven ... for you have said in your heart: I will ascend to Heaven, I will exalt my throne above the stars of God...I **will be like the most High**"* (Isaiah 14:12-15).

Matthew 7:13-14 reminds us to *"Enter through the narrow gate; for the way is broad that leads to destruction, and there are many who enter through it. For the gate is small and the way narrow that leads to life, and there are few who find it."*

The road of the wicked is well traveled, trampled, and smooth. It's easy to walk. The demonic realm doesn't try to knock you off this road, but you can expect to be tempted where your pride is concerned. This is the most destructive kind of attack. King Solomon warned that pride comes before a fall.

This type of attack can actually follow the moment you have done a good deed! Pride, or self-glorification, can become so strong it pulls you to a darker side. Or perhaps you, in pride, have relied on your own strength to control or handle a certain situation. We should never "try" in our own strength. Instead, we should turn to the Lord for help in every circumstance, as we are assured that *"I am able to do all things through the One who strengthens me"* (Philippians 4:13). Ephesians 6:10 urges us to *"Finally be strong in the Lord and in His mighty power."*

Satan's fall from Heaven was essentially his fourth and final fall. His first fall is found in Ezekiel 28:14-16. Jesus spoke of this in Luke 10:18 saying that He saw Satan fall "like lightning" from Heaven. His second fall was in Satan no longer having access to Heaven. Satan will fall a third time from his place on earth into the bottomless pit. His fourth, and final, fall will be from the bottomless pit to the lake of fire, his final destination (Revelation 20:10).

Why would a holy God create such a being? And why would God allow evil to continue? A jeweler presents a diamond to a buyer on a black cloth so the brilliance of the diamond shines forth even brighter. Paul, in Romans 8:28, tells us, *"And we know all things work together for good to those who love God, to those who are called according to His purpose."* So "all things," which would include evil, have a purpose.

God's plan for man and his salvation is centered in Jesus. The promised Messiah conquered sin and death. Satan's days are surely numbered.

Once you have given your life to the Lord, all you need do is rest. Jesus will sanctify and ready you to meet our Holy God, a God who loves you more than you can imagine. A God who is more than willing to share His home with man. *"No eye has seen, nor ear has heard, and no mind has imagined what God has prepared for those who love Him"* (1 Corinthians 2:9 NLT).

In the meantime, I urge you to pay attention to C.S. Lewis:

"There are only two kinds of people in the end: those who say to God, 'Thy will be done,' and those to whom God says, in the end, 'Thy will be done.' All that are in Hell choose it. Without that self-choice there could be no Hell. No soul that seriously and constantly desires joy will ever miss it. Those who seek find. To those who knock it will be opened."[21]

---

[21] C.S. Lewis, "The Great Divorce," (San Francisco; HarperSanFrancisco) 1973

CHAPTER TEN

HEAVEN: THE ULTIMATE RETIREMENT PLAN

"I once scorned ev'ry fearful thought of death,
When it was but the end of pulse and breath,
But now my eyes have seen that past the pain
There is a world that's waiting to be claimed.
Earthmaker, Holy, let me now depart,
For living's such a temporary art
And dying is but getting dressed for God
Our graves are merely doorways cut in sod."
—*Calvin Miller*

Just as we have no words to adequately describe the horrors and torture of Hell, we are powerless to express the glory, grandeur, and splendor of Heaven. Just as the atheists mentioned in the previous chapter were terrified by their glimpses into the darkness and anguish of Hell, the last words of those who trusted in Christ give us the exact opposite: an ecstatic foretaste of the delights of Heaven.

Denny Rainey, in his article, "Famous Last Words," published on Christianity.com, tells us, "Billy Graham notes that when the great saint Joseph Everett was dying, he said, 'GLORY! GLORY! GLORY!' and continued exclaiming 'GLORY!' for over twenty-five minutes until he was whisked away by angels to the gates of Heaven."[22]

It is well recorded that, a few hours before his death, the great evangelist Dwight L. Moody caught a glimpse of the magnificence and glory of Heaven. He awakened from sleep and said, "Earth recedes. Heaven opens before me. If this is death, it is sweet! There is no valley here. God is calling me, and I must go!"

His son, who stood at his bedside, said, "No, no, father. You are dreaming."

But Dr. Moody replied, "No, I am not dreaming. I have been within the gates: I have seen the children's faces." After a short time, he spoke once more, "This is my triumph; this is my coronation day! It is glorious!"

Recognized as one of the great Christian orators of the 20th century, Dr. R. G. Lee was known for painting vivid pictures with his words. It was said that Dr. Lee, through the Spirit of God, could make the invisible seem to be just in sight. He could dramatically portray the Lord and the eternal home of the saints of God. Yet when Dr. Lee was dying, he suddenly opened his eyes and said to his wife, "I see Heaven! Oh ... I didn't do it justice! I see JESUS! I didn't do HIM justice!"[23]

Great peace and hope can be found in the final, dying words of a Civil War general. Even with his death at hand, Thomas "Stonewall" Jackson seemed to convey a touch of humor and expectation, rather than a fear or dread of dying.

"I see from the number of physicians that you think my condition dangerous, but I thank God, if it is His will, that I am ready to go. It is the Lord's day; my wish is fulfilled. I have always desired

---

[22] https://www.christianity.com/christian-life/famous-last-words-11545269.html, accessed March 25, 2021

[23] http://www.liftingupjesus.com/Outlines/The Last Words of Saints and Sinners.html/ access March 25, 2021

to die on Sunday. Order A.P. Hill to prepare for action! Pass the infantry to the front rapidly! Tell Major Hawks…"

At this point, he stopped, leaving the sentence unfinished. Presently a smile of sweetness spread itself over his pale face, and he said quietly with an expression, as if of relief, "let us cross the river and rest under the shade of the trees."

William Allingham, the Irish Poet, on his deathbed said, "I see such things as you cannot imagine."

The last words of John Newton, the author of "Amazing Grace," were, "I am still in the land of the dying; I shall be in the land of the living soon."

How different are the final moments of those who believe and have received Jesus Christ as Lord and Savior from those who denied Him and chose to go their own way, which inevitably leads to eternity in Hell!

The previous chapter goes into great detail about the horrors of Hell. But what about the splendor of Heaven?

Depending on the translation, "Heaven" is mentioned as many as 327 times in the Old Testament and 255 times in the New Testament.[24] Thousands of books have been written on the subject with amazon.com listing over 60,000 books with "Heaven" in the title. While some of these are novels and others are not Biblically based, it's obvious that at least the concept of Heaven is a topic weighing heavily on the minds of many writers.

So what will it be like to spend eternity in Heaven? Thankfully, those who picture Heaven as a place where we will lie on fluffy clouds and play harps forever will find themselves mistaken. Admittedly, such an existence sounds incredibly boring. I assure you, Heaven will be anything but boring!

---

[24] www.reference.com/world-view/many-times-Heaven-mentioned-Bible-a401ce6e93dd2edf/accessed March 25, 2021

To be accurate and to correctly interpret what the Bible tells us about Heaven, we must first understand that when we typically talk about Heaven, we're thinking of the intermediate Heaven. That's the place we go when we die. It's the place we will live until our earthly bodies are resurrected. It's a beautiful place with no pain, no suffering, no crime, no poverty. A place where we will be reunited with loved ones and enjoy the presence of the Lord.

After the Second Coming of Christ, when He makes all things new — including a New Heaven and a New Earth — Scripture tells us we will live in a city designed and built by God Himself: *"For he was looking forward to the city with foundations, whose architect and builder is God ... For here we do not have an enduring city, but we are looking for the city that is to come"* (Hebrews 11:10; 13:14).

That city is further described in Revelation 21:18-23:

> *"The wall was made of jasper, and the city of pure gold, as pure as glass. The foundations of the city walls were decorated with every kind of precious stone. The first foundation was jasper, the second sapphire, the third agate, the fourth emerald, the fifth onyx, the sixth ruby, the seventh chrysolite, the eighth beryl, the ninth topaz, the tenth turquoise, the eleventh jacinth, and the twelfth amethyst. The twelve gates were twelve pearls, each gate made of a single pearl. The great street of the city was of gold, as pure as transparent glass.*
>
> *I did not see a Temple in the city, because the Lord God Almighty and the Lamb are its Temple. The city does not need the sun or the moon to shine on it, for the glory of God gives it light, and the Lamb is its lamp."*

It is clear that the magnificence of Heaven is far beyond anything we can comprehend with our finite minds. But what is most amazing is that we will live in the presence of God —Father, Son, and Holy Spirit.

There will be no curse on the New Earth. God will be permanently enthroned in the city, and we will serve Him (Revelation 22:3). Satan and all those who refused Christ as Savior will be banished.

Perhaps you are going through seemingly unbearable circumstances in your life and, as a result, feel hopeless. It may feel like you are living through Hell on earth. But the Bible tells us all of this life's suffering pales when we consider the joys and splendor that await us in Heaven. It all comes into perspective.

C.S. Lewis, scholar and author of "The Chronicles of Narnia," and multiple Christian works, writes:

"Both good and evil, when they are full grown, become retrospective...That is what mortals misunderstand. They say of some temporary suffering, 'No future bliss can make up for it,' not knowing that Heaven, once attained, will work backwards and turn even that agony into a glory. And of some sinful pleasure they say 'Let me but have this and I'll take the consequences': little dreaming how damnation will spread back and back into their past and contaminate the pleasure of the sin."

Our perfect new world will be filled with things we are familiar with. We can expect to see people and houses, trees and flowers, air and water, and even streets and buildings. But all these things will be a far better version than anything we have experienced in this life.

We will have new bodies, and these bodies will be without pain, disease, or weakness. We will never grow old or be subject to death. And our minds and attitudes will be made new.

All the citizens of Heaven will find our greatest fulfillment and satisfaction in worshiping, thanking, and exploring our God. His glory and power will continually be revealed to us so that we will forever be in awe of who He is. We will see His beauty reflected in His creation and in those who inhabit Heaven.

The Bible is clear that we will rule and reign with Christ. We will have work to do, but that work will no longer be under the curse. Can you imagine having a job you can't wait to do? A job with goals and plans where you can work in peace and joy amidst fellow workers who enjoy each other and work without jealousy or competition.

While Hell and its torments are very real — and indescribably horrific — the good news is that the Lord wants us to be in Heaven with Him. He has given everyone the roadmap and the free will to choose.

God sacrificed His own Son to provide the way to eternal joy. And He can't make our entrance to Heaven any easier. As the old hymn says, the only thing required of us is to "trust and obey."

Once we realize we are in control of nothing, that we can do nothing to add to the finished work of the cross, then we are ready to receive and be part of God's plan. His plan is based totally on faith.

"As surely as I live, declares the Sovereign Lord, I take no pleasure in the death of the wicked, but rather that they turn from their ways and live. Turn! Turn from your evil ways! Why will you die ...?" (Ezekiel 33:11)

King Solomon's final thoughts remind us that there is one truth no one can deny: everyone dies. Hebrews 9:27 emphasizes the point saying, *"And insomuch as it is appointed for men to die once and after that comes judgement."*

In his sermon, "The Ever Changing Seasons Of Life," based on Ecclesiastes 3:1-8, Pastor Victor Haynes tells us "... all of human existence, when lived apart from God, is frustrating and unsatisfactory. All of the pleasures and material things of life, when sought for their own sake, bring nothing but unhappiness and a sense of futility.

"The primary aim of the author [King Solomon] is to show from personal experience that all earthly goals and blessings, when pursued as an end in themselves, lead to dissatisfaction and emptiness."[25]

No one can find true and complete happiness in wisdom, money, pleasure, or power. As Solomon would say, it's like striving after the wind. He goes on further to say the dead know nothing, the food and flowers left at the grave are meaningless.

There are no more choices once a person is declared dead. No more chances for salvation. All earthly opportunities are gone forever.

Isaac Watts (1674-1748) an English minister and theologian, credited with 750 hymns, including "O God, Our Help in Ages Past," wrote these glorious words regarding Heaven:

"How divinely full of glory and pleasure shall that hour be when all the millions of mankind that have been redeemed by the blood of the Lamb of God shall meet together and stand around Him, with every tongue and every heart full of joy and praise!

"How astonishing will be the glory and the joy of that day when all the saints shall join together in one common song of gratitude and love, and of everlasting thankfulness to this Redeemer! With that unknown delight, and inexpressible satisfaction, shall all that are saved from the ruins of sin and Hell address the Lamb that was slain, and rejoice in His presence!"

Your life is a journey only you can take, and you can choose to go it alone or walk with Christ. The choice lies in your acknowledgement of God and submitting to His perfect will.

Jesus Himself extends the invitation to join Him in Heaven by believing in Him:

> *"Do not let your hearts be troubled. You believe in God; believe also in me. My Father's house has many rooms; if that were not so, would I have told you that I am going*

---

[25] https://www.sermoncentral.com/sermons/the-ever-changing-seasons-of-life-victor-haynes-sermon-on-change-203056/ accessed March 25, 2021

there to prepare a place for you? And if I go and prepare a place for you, I will come back and take you to be with me that you also may be where I am." (John 14:1-3)

Our lives are brief. Choose life. Accept Jesus Christ as Lord and Savior and receive Heaven as your eternal reward.

CPSIA information can be obtained
at www.ICGtesting.com
Printed in the USA
BVHW071743060821
613849BV00007B/207